DR. YASH

THE WORLD IN TURMOIL

CITI OF BOOKS

Copyright © 2024 by Dr. Yash P. Soni

All rights reserved. No part of this publication may be reproduced, distributed, or transmitted in any form or by any means, including photocopying, recording, or other electronic or mechanical methods, without the prior written permission of the copyright owner and the publisher, except in the case of brief quotations embodied in critical reviews and certain other noncommercial uses permitted by copyright law. For permission requests, write to the publisher, addressed "Attention: Permissions Coordinator," at the address below.

CITIOFBOOKS, INC.
3736 Eubank NE Suite A1
Albuquerque, NM 87111-3579
www.citiofbooks.com
Hotline: 1 (877) 389-2759
Fax: 1 (505) 930-7244

Ordering Information:

Quantity sales. Special discounts are available on quantity purchases by corporations, associations, and others. For details, contact the publisher at the address above.

Printed in the United States of America.

ISBN-13:	Softcover	979-8-89391-333-0
	Ebook	979-8-89391-334-7

Library of Congress Control Number: 2024919365

Table of Contents

ACKNOWLEDGEMENT 1

Preface 3

Introduction 8

Chapter 1
A Decade of Conflict – the War in Russia and Ukraine 9

Chapter 2
Middle East Unrest: Israel-Palestine Conflict Overview of the Israel-Palestine conflict 21

Chapter 3:
China's Ascendancy: Regional Ambitions and Global Impact 39

Chapter 4
Indian Politics and Economic Outlook 51

Chapter 5
Pakistan's Elections and Economic Challenges 65

Chapter 6
South American Shifts: Brazil, Mexico, and Changing Dynamics 81

Chapter 7
Western Democracies: Elections and Global Leadership 92

Chapter 8
The Erosion of Democracy under Trump, Putin, and Other Power-Hungry Leaders 97

Chapter 9
The current Shocking Twists in U.S. Politics: Assassination Attempt on Trump and Biden's Unexpected Exit from the Presidential Race" 118

References 133

ACKNOWLEDGEMENT

THE WORLD IN TURMOIL

As I pen my thoughts in "World in Turmoil" it is essential to recognize the many individuals and in fluences that have guided me through this exploration of the pressing issue facing our world today.!!!

First and foremost, I extend my deepest Gratitude to my team whose unwavering support and patience provided me the strength to tackle this challenging topic.

A special thanks to my friends and colleagues with whom I have had long discussions on this topic and their perspectives have enriched, the content of this book.

Their passion and desire for understanding the complexities of our world has inspired me to delve deeper into the issue that matter. I acknowledge the contributions of Mary Kenneth and Uma Anand for their scholarly insights, I thank for providing resources and research support. Having known Mary Kenneth and Uma for the past so many years, I have consistently admired their extensive knowledge across various subjects and their unwavering dedication to excellence. Mary suggestions, and support have significantly shaped the content of The World in Turmoil. Thank you, Mary, for your exceptional contribution and for being an inspiring collaborator throughout this journey.

I am also grateful to the countless voices and activist advocating for change in our world. Their courage and commitment to social justice and peace have not only informed my writing but have also ignited a passion within me to raise awareness and provoke thought through this book. A heartfelt acknowledgment goes to the readers who seek to understand the complexities of our times. It is my hope that this work resonates with you and sparks conversation that led to meaningful actions.

In a world filled with turmoil, may we find the resolve to confront our challenges together. Fostering empathy, understanding, and resilience.

Finally, I extend my gratitude to my readers. It is my hope that this book resonates with you and prompts reflection and dialogue about the ever-changing world we inhabit.

May we seek understanding and strive for a more harmonious future. Thank you for accompanying me on this journey.

Hope you will enjoy this book good read before the new topics arrives at my desk. Reading this book as what is happening in the world today amazing ??

Suggestions and feedback are always welcome from my readers, Yash@Yashgolfwear.com I am always interested to listen to my readers for future improvement.

Preface

The World in Turmoil Preface

Imagine a world where countries' borders are always shifting, cities that used to be thriving are now in ruins, and the news is filled with constant reports of wars and other emergencies. If I told you that this is not just a possible future but the present situation for millions of people around the world, would you believe me? What means did we use to get to where we are now, and more importantly, what direction are we moving in?

Investigating the stories behind the news reveals the complexity of a world perpetually undergoing upheaval and change.

The objective

Understanding the connections between conflicts, political disruptions, and shifting power dynamics is crucial during this unprecedented period of global unrest. It was my goal in writing this book to give a thorough look at the world's most important problems, going beyond basic facts to help readers get a deeper understanding of the things that affect the way things are now.

My passion propels me to demonstrate the interconnectedness of seemingly disparate events and places. By reading about the causes and effects of these global issues, I hope to make my readers more informed and caring. This book is more than just a record of terrible things that happened. It's an invitation to actively and carefully learn more about the complicated things in our world.

My ultimate goal is to achieve consciousness and a sense of importance. Understanding the complexities of global turmoil in the past and present is critical to making good decisions about the future and working for peace, stability, and cooperation. My hope is that this book will start important conversations and lead people to take action that will make the world a better place for everyone.

Background

As a long-time journalist covering global conflicts and political upheavals, I have seen firsthand the terrible effects of war, unstable economies, and dictatorships. My time in Ukraine, as well as my time working in politics in Washington, D.C., and Beijing, has affected my book. Having traversed these challenging regions, I have gained a fresh outlook on the interconnectedness of global issues and the criticality of comprehending and addressing them.

Book structure

Join us as we explore the complex fabric of modern society. Each thread tells a story of struggle, hope, and change. This book's goal is not just to tell you about events; it also wants to help you understand the deeper forces that are shaping our global environment. As we deal with wars, political unrest, and shifting power structures, our goal is to give you a full picture of the problems and opportunities that make up our time.

Many conflicts and chaos have plagued the world recently. The global stage appears to be becoming more unstable as a result of regional conflicts, economic downturns, and political unrest. In addition to happening alone, these conflicts are worsening each other. Understanding these dynamics is important for anyone who wants to understand the world we live in now.

In the next few chapters, we'll talk about some of the most important conflicts and power struggles of our time. Each chapter of the book goes into detail about a different area or theme, looking at the causes, important events, and possible future trends. Our aim is to present a comprehensive picture that demonstrates the interconnectedness of seemingly disparate elements, unveiling a multifaceted network of interactions and consequences.

Chapter 1: War in Russia and Ukraine: A Decade of Conflict

The ongoing fighting between Russia and Ukraine marks the start of our expedition. The ongoing conflict, which has been going on for more than ten years, has completely changed the political landscape of Eastern Europe and the surrounding areas. We investigate where this conflict originated, tracing its historical tensions and looking at how international actors got involved. Our goal is to give you a better understanding of the ongoing war's effects on people and the government by looking closely at important events like the annexation of Crimea and the most recent military offensives.

Chapter 2: Middle East Unrest: Israel-Palestine Conflict

Now, let's talk about the Middle East. The conflict between Israel and Palestine is still one of the most complicated and emotional in recent memory. This chapter talks about the conflict's historical roots, how regional and global politics have affected it, and how the fighting has changed people's daily lives. We examine the ongoing peace efforts, the challenges faced, and the optimism for a potential solution.

Chapter 3: China's Ascendancy: Regional Ambitions and Global Impact

Moving on from the Middle East, we now look at Asia, where China's rise to become a major world power is fundamentally changing the political landscape around the world. This chapter looks at China's goals in the region, including its assertive actions in the South China Sea and the Belt and Road Initiative. We also look at the effects of China's economic and military growth on the rest of the world, including how other countries have responded to this new situation.

Chapter 4: Indian Politics, 2024 Election and Economic Outlook

India is the world's largest democracy, but things are going badly now that the 2024 elections are over. This chapter examines the political climate, the well-known individuals involved, and the issues that have arisen and dominated the election debate. We also look at India's economic future, taking into account the challenges and opportunities that this rapidly growing and important country faces now that its government has changed.

Chapter 5: Pakistan's Future Elections and Economic Challenges

Pakistan faces numerous political and economic challenges due to its proximity to the border. This chapter looks at the complicated nature of Pakistan's upcoming elections, how the military will be involved, and the economic problems that are stopping the country from moving forward. We look at how a country that is critical to the region's safety and progress can become more stable and grow its economy.

Chapter 6: Western Democracies: Elections and Global Leadership

Looking at the Western parts of the world, we see how democratic systems are doing in North America and Europe right now. This chapter is primarily about the most recent elections, the rise of populism as a political force, and the problems that traditional leadership is facing. We examine how these democratic countries deal with disagreements within their own borders and fit into a rapidly changing global system.

Chapter 7: South American Shifts: Brazil, Mexico, and Changing Dynamics

The political and economic situations in South America are changing right now. Brazil and Mexico, two major countries in the region, dominate this chapter. We look at the recent changes in politics, economic policies, and social movements that are shaping the continent. This expedition gives us a quick look into the possible future of a place that is full of useful resources and untapped potential.

Chapter 8: The Erosion of Democracy under Trump, Putin, and Other Power-Hungry Leaders

The last part of our work is about a worrying trend happening around the world: democratic systems are slowly falling apart. We look at how authoritarian leaders like Donald Trump and Vladimir Putin have become more powerful, putting democratic institutions and principles at risk. Through case studies and comparative studies, we look at the methods these leaders use to strengthen their power and the effects these methods have on global democracy.

A Decree to Act

As we near the conclusion of this journey, we contemplate the connections between these changes and conflicts. Understanding the forces behind the world's constant change is crucial to surviving. We hope that this book will help you understand the complicated world around us better and inspire you to deal with these issues with critical thinking and wisdom.

Thank you for choosing to join us in this project. Let's look at, understand, and find solutions to the problems that affect our global society as a whole.

Introduction

Worldwide wars and conflicts are causing substantial tensions and upheaval, affecting the local areas and having global repercussions. The prolonged violence in Syria, the instability in Yemen, and the persistent tensions in Ukraine have extensive repercussions. The relocation of millions of people has resulted in a refugee crisis that is putting a strain on resources and challenging international cooperation. Moreover, these conflicts frequently worsen preexisting socio-economic inequalities, leading to increased hatred and creating a conducive environment for extremism and radicalization.

Furthermore, the increase in violent conflicts leads to an unstable atmosphere that endangers regional stability and obstructs diplomatic attempts for peace and collaboration. Violence spreading across borders via terrorism and insurgency makes it more difficult to control and settle conflicts. Continual warfare has negative economic impacts by disrupting trade routes, deterring investment, and obstructing development, which leads to persistent poverty and underdevelopment in impacted areas. Moreover, the arms trade thrives during these crises, sustaining a harmful cycle of bloodshed and financial gain. Ongoing crises on the geopolitical stage are used as flashpoints for competition and proxy warfare between global powers, leading to increased tensions and a greater danger of broader conflict. In a globally connected world, the repercussions of these wars extend beyond their initial locations, underscoring the critical necessity for unified international actions to tackle their underlying reasons and foster enduring peace. Understanding the consequences of global wars highlights the interdependence of nations and the collective duty of the worldwide community to maintain peace, security, and human rights. The importance of working together to tackle the underlying reasons for conflict, encourage reconciliation, and establish lasting peace for current and future generations should addressed. In this investigation, we look at the complex circumstances of ongoing global wars, their deep effects, and the chaos they cause. Here, we will establish how important it is to understand and deal with their wide-ranging effects. We invite you to accompany us as we explore the complex web of conflict in search of an understanding of its global impact on society.

Chapter 1: A Decade of Conflict – the War in Russia and Ukraine

1•Background Of the Conflict Between Russia and Ukraine

Russia and Ukraine are at odds with each other over a long-running geopolitical war that has historical, cultural, and strategic aspects. To understand its history, we must go back hundreds of years and look at important events in modern times. Russia and Ukraine have had a complicated connection over the years, with times of tension and centuries of shared history. In the past, Ukraine was part of the Russian Empire until the fall of the Tsarist government in 1917. It was then often called "Little Russia." After the Bolshevik Revolution and the Russian Civil War, Ukraine had a short period of freedom in 1918. In 1922, it became part of the Soviet Union.

During the Soviet era, Ukraine went through times of oppression, such as the terrible Holodomor famine in the 1930s, which was caused by Soviet policies. But there were also times when it had some cultural and political freedom within the Soviet system. When the Soviet Union broke up in 1991, it was a turning point for Ukraine. It claimed independence and became a sovereign state. Ukraine has had a hard time finding its national identity and place on the world stage since it became independent. Different groups of people in the country have strong opinions about its geopolitical orientation.

Some want closer links with Russia, while others want to join Western organizations like the European Union and NATO.

The Euromaidan protests in Kyiv in 2014 became one of the main points of conflict between Russia and Ukraine. There were protests when Viktor Yanukovych, President at the time, decided to back out of a deal to join the E.U. in favor of closer ties with Russia. This turned into a full-blown revolution, which got rid of Yanukovych. When Russia took over Crimea in March 2014, things got even worse between the two countries. After a controversial vote that was called illegitimate by the rest of the world, Russia officially took over Crimea, which Ukraine and most of the rest of the world still don't accept. At the same time, there was chaos in eastern Ukraine, especially in the Donetsk and Luhansk regions, where pro-Russian separatists took over government offices and declared themselves independent "people's republics." When the conflict turned into an actual uprising, both sides started using weapons, killing thousands of people and causing a lot of pain for civilians.

During the war in eastern Ukraine, there have been claims that Russia sent military aid to the separatist forces, including weapons, equipment, and people. Russia says it has nothing to do with the conflict and instead calls it a civil war, saying that Ukraine is violating the rights of Russian-speaking communities. There have been ongoing efforts to end the war, including diplomatic efforts like the Minsk agreements, which France and Germany negotiated in 2014 and 2015. But implementation has been spotty, with ceasefires often broken and peace talks stuck because of mistrust and political maneuvering. The conflict between Russia and Ukraine isn't just a disagreement between the two countries; it also affects the safety and stability of Europe as a whole. It shows how hard it is to deal with complicated historical legacies, racial tensions, and geopolitical rivalries in the post-Soviet world. As long as the conflict lasts, both sides need to work together on diplomatic issues, de-escalation, and a peaceful settlement to stop more deaths and instability in the area.

2 •Recent Russia Vs Ukraine War Developments and Escalations in The Last Two Years

The ongoing dispute between Russia and Ukraine has experienced numerous escalations and developments over the last two years, which have served to heighten tensions and complicate an already complex situation. Amidst the backdrop of ongoing diplomatic efforts, intermittent ceasefires, and ongoing violence in eastern Ukraine, these events have transpired.

An early 2022 escalation of hostilities, characterized by a surge in ceasefire violations and intensified combat in the Donbas region, constituted a significant development in the conflict. Clashes broke out between Ukrainian forces and separatists supported by Russia, leading to an increase in human casualties and suffering. A renewed demand for a diplomatic resolution was issued in response to the escalation, and concerns were expressed regarding the ceasefire agreements' fragility. Early in 2021, a more noteworthy occurrence was the Russian military's expansion towards the Ukrainian border, which sparked concerns about the possibility of a massive offensive. In addition to military exercises and provocative maneuvers, the troop buildup escalated tensions between Russia and Ukraine and with the international community. Although Russia defended the troop deployment as a defensive strategy, it was universally perceived as a coercive maneuver to pressure Ukraine and its Western allies.

The conflict has experienced diplomatic maneuvering and geopolitical developments that have influenced the relations between Russia, Ukraine, and other significant actors, in addition to military escalations. An instance of such a development occurred in January 2021 with the inauguration of Joe Biden as the President of the United States. The Biden administration marked a shift in U.S. policy toward Ukraine by adopting a more assertive posture toward Russia and reaffirming support for Ukraine's sovereignty and territorial integrity. The change in rhetoric and approach has ramifications for diplomatic endeavors to resolve the dispute and has played a role in the realignment of regional power structures.

Moreover, advancements in the broader geopolitical sphere, such as Russia's tense relations with the European Union (E.U.) and NATO, have affected the conflict. The deterioration of Russia-EU relations has been exacerbated by ongoing disputes concerning human rights, energy supplies, and cybersecurity, all of which have repercussions for efforts to resolve the conflict in Ukraine. Disagreements regarding military deployments, armaments control, and strategic competition in Eastern Europe have similarly maintained elevated tension levels between Russia and NATO.

In light of the circumstances above—including heightened military operations, strategic diplomacy, and geopolitical strains—the ongoing dispute between Russia and Ukraine remains a major obstacle to regional and global security. Achieving a peaceful resolution to the conflict continues to be challenging, impeded by entrenched animosity, conflicting interests, and the lack of a comprehensive framework for negotiations. As the ongoing conflict enters its eighth year, an increasingly critical international community is needed to reinstate diplomatic efforts, implement de-escalation strategies, and pressure the parties involved to preserve sovereignty and territorial integrity.

3 •Impact Of War on Ukraine and Its Infrastructure

The war has had a profound and multifaceted effect on Ukraine's infrastructure, affecting numerous sectors vital to the economy and society. The adverse effects of conflict have hindered the nation's progress, exacerbating preexisting difficulties and affecting various sectors including healthcare, education, transportation, and utilities.

The devastation of transportation networks, such as airports, roads, bridges, and railways, has been one of the most obvious and immediate consequences of the conflict in Ukraine. The movement of goods and people have been disrupted by infrastructure damage, which has impeded economic and commercial activity and complicated the delivery of humanitarian assistance. Additionally, communities have been isolated as a result of the devastation of vital transportation arteries, which has exacerbated social and economic disparities and impeded access to essential services.

Furthermore, the energy infrastructure of Ukraine has been severely impacted by the conflict, specifically in the eastern regions that have been the site of hostilities. Enforced by the destruction of power plants, substations, and transmission lines, widespread electricity outages have ensued, placing additional strain on the economy and compounding the difficulties endured by the populace. As a consequence of the interruptions in energy supplies, heating has been compromised throughout the severe winter season, presenting further obstacles to the resilience and welfare of the populace. The water and sanitation systems are additional critical components of the war-hit infrastructure of Ukraine. The compromise of access to pure water and sanitation services for millions of individuals due to damage to water treatment plants, pipelines, and sewage networks has increased the likelihood of waterborne diseases and public health emergencies. Water sources have been further contaminated due to infrastructure destruction, contributing to environmental degradation and increased health risks for the communities impacted.

In addition, the healthcare infrastructure in Ukraine has been significantly impacted by the conflict, as evidenced by the overcrowding of victims and the interruption of medical provisions. The destruction or damage to hospitals and clinics in conflict-affected regions has restricted civilians' access to vital medical services and exacerbated their suffering. The insufficiency of personnel, medical supplies, and apparatus has further compounded the difficulties encountered by the healthcare system, impeding its capacity to address the demands of the populace adequately.

The conflict has severely impacted education infrastructure; due to security concerns, schools, universities, and educational facilities have been damaged or forced to close. Depriving millions of children and young people of access to learning opportunities, the disruption of education has exacerbated social inequalities and perpetuated cycles of poverty and underdevelopment. In addition to undermining the nation's long-term recovery and reconstruction prospects, the devastation of educational infrastructure has deprived future generations of the knowledge and abilities required to rebuild their communities and contribute to the nation's development.

Furthermore, the repercussions of the conflict on Ukraine's infrastructure transcend physical destruction, encompassing far-reaching economic and social implications that resonate across society. Investments have been impeded, economic activity has been disrupted, and the devastation of infrastructure has hampered efforts to rebuild and revitalize affected communities. Additionally, the destruction of infrastructure assets has hindered the nation's productive capacity, which has impeded its ability to generate income, create employment, and provide for its citizens' livelihoods.

Furthermore, apart from the aforementioned immediate consequences, the infrastructure devastation in Ukraine has resulted in enduring ramifications that have further exacerbated issues such as poverty, inequality, and social exclusion. Reconstructing and restoring infrastructure after armed conflict presents insurmountable obstacles that must be surmounted with considerable capital, resources, and knowledge. Notwithstanding these obstacles, the restoration of infrastructure offers a prospect to rectify the harm caused by conflict and construct more effectively, thereby promoting inclusiveness, sustainability, and resilience in Ukraine's trajectory of progress.

In summary, the conflict has had a profound and extensive effect on Ukraine's infrastructure, encompassing various critical sectors essential for the operation of society and the economy. Consequences of the devastation of infrastructure in education, healthcare, transportation, energy, and water have exacerbated humanitarian crises and impeded the nation's progress. Infrastructure restoration and rebuilding will be critical for the recovery and reconstruction of Ukraine in the aftermath of the conflict. This will require the government, international community, and civil society to collaborate to address the complex challenges of war and pave the way for a more resilient and prosperous future.

4•The Effects of Sanctions and Trade Restrictions on Russia

Sanctions and trade restrictions have profoundly and extensively affected Russia, influenced numerous economic sectors and molded the nation's geopolitical terrain. Russia, being a significant player on the international stage and possessing one of the largest economies globally, has encountered considerable obstacles due to the sanctions imposed by the international community in retaliation for its activities in Ukraine, Syria, and various other geopolitical conflicts.

The Russian economy, specifically its petroleum and financial sectors, has experienced one of the most immediate repercussions of the sanctions. Due to the sanctions imposed, Russia's access to international financial markets has been restricted, limiting its capacity to finance investments, raise capital, and conduct transactions in foreign currencies. As a result, capital fled Russia, and the ruble depreciated, which increased inflationary pressures and diminished the purchasing power of Russian citizens.

Furthermore, critical sectors of the Russian economy, such as the energy industry, which is pivotal to the nation's economic output and export revenues, have been singled out by sanctions. The advancement of novel initiatives and the modernization of preexisting infrastructure have been impeded due to limitations on investment, technology transfers, and collaboration with Russian energy corporations. Consequently, Russia's capability to exploit its extensive natural gas and oil reserves and sustain its status as a preeminent energy exporter has been compromised.

In addition, sanctions have discouraged multinational corporations and financial institutions from entering the Russian market out of concern for legal compliance and reputational risk, which has a debilitating effect on foreign investment in Russia. Consequently, Russia's endeavors to foster technological progress, attract foreign investment, and diversify its economy have been impeded, particularly in critical industries like finance, telecommunications, and manufacturing.

Furthermore, sanctions have exerted geopolitical repercussions on Russia, influencing its diplomatic ties with other nations, global strategic standing, and economic ramifications. Relations between Russia and the West have deteriorated due to sanctions imposed by Western powers, including the European Union and the United States. This has fueled mutual mistrust, hatred, and confrontation.

Moreover, preexisting tensions between Russia and neighboring countries have been further intensified by sanctions, specifically in Eastern Europe and the former Soviet Union. Russia's assertive foreign policy and military interventions in these regions have engendered apprehensions regarding their intentions and aspirations. The implementation of sanctions has exacerbated divisions and fostered an atmosphere of insecurity and instability in the area, further polarizing regional dynamics.

In addition, the Russian populace has been adversely affected by the social and humanitarian repercussions of sanctions, which have exacerbated poverty, inequality, and social exclusion. Job losses, wage stagnation, and a decline in living standards have occurred a great number of Russians due to the economic depression brought about by sanctions, especially those whose livelihoods depend on sectors impacted by sanctions, such as energy, finance, and manufacturing. Social discontent and political unrest have been further exacerbated by the decline in economic opportunities, thereby presenting obstacles to Russia's internal stability and governance.

The Russian government has implemented various measures in reaction to the sanctions to mitigate their consequences and protect the nation's interests. Some of these measures include strengthening domestic industries, diversifying trade and investment partners, and pursuing closer economic and strategic ties with other countries, particularly Asia and the Middle East. Furthermore, Russia has implemented alternative financial mechanisms to bypass sanctions, including barter arrangements and using cryptocurrencies. It has also strengthened economic ties with nations subject to comparable sanctions, including Venezuela and Iran. Furthermore, Russia has engaged in diplomatic endeavors to contest the validity of sanctions and garner backing from countries that share its stance, presenting itself as a target of interference and aggression from the West.

Notwithstanding these endeavors, sanctions continue to significantly impact Russia's economy and geopolitical standing, thereby presenting obstacles to its sustained progress and stability. A climate of economic and political unpredictability has prevailed in Russia due to the enduring nature of sanctions and the ambiguity surrounding their future course. This has impeded innovation, investment, and reform, which is essential for addressing structural deficiencies and fostering sustainable growth.

In summary, sanctions and trade restrictions have had far-reaching and diverse consequences for Russia, affecting many facets, including the economy, society, and geopolitics. Despite Russia's efforts to alleviate the repercussions of sanctions via various strategies and measures, their persistent enforcement presents substantial obstacles to the nation's economic progress, geopolitical aspirations, and internal harmony. The ongoing impasse between Russia and the West is expected to have lasting repercussions on Russia and the international community, significantly influencing future global relations and dynamics.

5•New Sanctions In 2024 And Their Impacts on Russia

The United States issued a comprehensive list of new sanctions and export designations on February 23, 2024, marking the second anniversary of Russia's invasion of Ukraine and in retaliation for the death of Russian opposition leader Alexei Navalny. The list included Russia's financial infrastructure, military-industrial complex, and third parties that assist Russia in evading U.S. export controls and sanctions, among other entities. Furthermore, the United States government issued a risk assessment titled "Risks and Considerations for Conducting Business in the Russian Federation and Russia-Occupied Territories of Ukraine" to underscore the substantial hazards associated with engaging in lawful commerce with or within Russia. Although the United States has implemented substantial sanctions and other limitations against Russia for the past two years, the designation of hundreds of individuals and entities on Friday is meant to signal that Russia will continue to be a jurisdiction subject to substantial trade restrictions for the foreseeable future and to demonstrate enduring resolve.

Designations of Sanctions

The U.S. Department of the Treasury stated in a press release announcing the new sanctions that the Office of Foreign Assets Control ("OFAC") was "sanctioning nearly 300 individuals and entities," including "hundreds of entities operating in Russia's military-industrial base and other critical sectors; a major cog in Russia's financial infrastructure; and more than two dozen third-country sanctions evaders from Europe, East Asia, Central Asia, and the Middle East."

A. Financial Sanctions on Services

OFAC has imposed sanctions on numerous of Russia's largest financial institutions, including the Central Bank of Russia, PJSC Sberbank, and VTB Bank PJSC, among others, over the past two years. Sanctions have had a substantial effect by impeding the ability of U.S. citizens to engage in transactions with Russian counterparties, including those not subject to sanctions.

OFAC imposed additional sanctions on twenty-one entities functioning in Russia's financial sector even though the list of non-sanctioned financial institutions operating in Russia was already short.

1. Initially, sanctions were levied by OFAC against the state-owned National Payment Card System Joint Stock Company ("NSPK"), which is responsible for the operation of the Russian National Payment System. The Organization of American Activities Concerned (OFAC) concluded that NSPK assisted Russia in evading sanctions and emphasized that the designation was designed to thwart Russian attempts to "reestablish severed ties with the international financial system."

2. Second, to further restrict Russia's financial system, OFAC added to the List of Specially Designated Nationals (the "SDN List") six fintech companies (including developers of economic systems, cryptography tools, and software), five investment companies and firms, and nine financial institutions headquartered in Russia.

B. Sanctions on Industrial and Military Bases

The most extensive classification of recent sanctions levied by OFAC pertains to various entities engaged in operations within Russia's military-industrial complex. "[A]s Russia's overheating war economy continues to cannibalize non-defense-related production at the expense of future economic prospects for the Russian people, an increasing number of entities across Russia are contributing directly or indirectly to Russia's war machine," according to OFAC. This increases the likelihood that additional designations will be issued in the future.

Weapons manufacturers, additive manufacturing (e.g., 3D printing) parties, machine tool and metalworking equipment developers, industrial chemical (e.g., lubricant, coolant) and semiconductor and electronic component manufacturers, industrial automation (including artificial intelligence development) parties, optics designers (e.g., thermal imaging), and semiconductor and electronic component manufacturers are classified as entities designated to the SDN List.

C. Shipping Sanctions

Joint Stock corporation Sovcomflot ("Sovcomflot"), the fleet operator and state-owned shipping corporation of Russia, and fourteen of its vessels were placed on the SDN List by OFAC. Sovcomflot was also subject to Executive Order 14024's Directive 3, which prohibits all dealings in, financing provision for, and other transactions involving new debt with a maturity of more than fourteen days or new equity issued by Sovcomflot after the date of sanctions implementation. These sanctions are intended to increase Russia's expenses and enforce the price cap on Russian crude. Nevertheless, the initial consequences of these sanctions will be partially alleviated through the utilization of general licenses granted by OFAC about the designation (expounded upon subsequently).

D. Sanctions Evaders

Over the past year, OFAC has improved its strategy for imposing sanctions on Russia by focusing on third-party groups that help Russia get around the strict sanctions put in place by the U.S. and its partners:

3. OFAC found several companies in the People's Republic of China that sent important technology to Russia. They also found a finance network run by Rheingold Edelmetall AG in Liechtenstein that was working with metals companies in Russia to avoid controls on that part of the Russian economy.

4. OFAC found that PJSC TransContainer, a freight forwarder, was involved in the Russian arms trade. They also found that technology exporters based in Serbia were sending goods and equipment to Russian electronics companies and that manufacturers and logistics companies from other countries were also involved.

5. Another thing OFAC looked at was a network that it thinks Russia has used to get robotic aerial vehicles (UAVs) from Iran. The Joint Stock Company Special Economic Zone of Industrial Production Alabuga was part of this network.

E. General Licenses

In connection with the new designations, OFAC granted four general licenses, the majority of which focus on permitting the winding down of transactions with newly designated parties:

6. According to General License No. 88A, parties have until 12:01 a.m. EDT on April 8, 2024, to close transactions with 18 selected sanctions targets, which include NSPK, Sovcomflot, and certain manufacturing enterprises, investment firms, and logistics providers.

7. According to General License No. 89, parties have until 12:01 a.m. EDT on April 8, 2024, to close transactions with eight separately sanctioned Russian financial institutions.

8. According to General License No. 90, parties have until 12:01 a.m. EDT on April 8, 2024, to wind down debt or equity transactions involving six identified sanctions targets.

9. According to General License No. 91A, parties have until 12:01 a.m. EDT on May 23, 2024, to participate in vessel-related transactions (such as safe docking and anchoring, crew health and safety, or emergency repairs) with six specified companies, including Sovcomflot.

10. According to General License No. 92, parties have until 12:01 a.m. EDT on April 8, 2024, to deliver and offload goods from boats classified on the SDN List because of their link to Sovcomflot.

11. Transactions forbidden by General License No. 93 involving vessels blocked simply due to Sovcomflot's ownership involvement and not individually designated to the SDN List are permitted.

F. Export Limitations

The announcement of the new sanctions levied by OFAC occurred in conjunction with measures taken by the Bureau of Industry and Security ("BIS") of the U.S. Department of Commerce.

1. Entity List Designations

The BIS designated 93 entities to the Entity List under 95 entries (considering certain entities that operate in multiple jurisdictions).

This designation restricts the flow of export administration regulations ("EAR")-required products or technology to the targeted entities. Russia is home to sixty-three (63) of the newly designated entities, Turkey to sixteen (16), China to eight, the United Arab Emirates to four, the Kyrgyz Republic to two, and India and South Korea to one each. Over fifty percent of these entities will also be classified as Russian-Belarusian military end users, subject to overlapping supplementary export restrictions.

2. Modification to the List of Common High-Priority Items

BIS has identified "common high priority items," denoted by six-digit Harmonized System ("H.S.") identifiers, that Russia intends to acquire for its weapons programs in collaboration with close U.S. allies, including Japan, the European Union, and the United Kingdom. These items comprise both those subject to EAR export controls and those categorized as EAR99 but regulated by industry-specific export controls. The Common High Priority Items List is intended to guide exporters regarding goods with the highest probability of diversion to Russia.

Chapter 2: Middle East Unrest: Israel-Palestine Conflict Overview of the Israel-Palestine conflict

For many decades, this multifaceted war between Israel and Palestine has been the focus of attention all across the world. The origins of the conflict can be traced back to the late 19th and early 20th centuries, when Zionism, a movement that advocated for establishing a Jewish state in Palestine, which was then under Ottoman administration, was at its height. The United Nations suggested a partition plan in 1947 to divide Palestine into two distinct states: one for Jews and one for Arabs. Nevertheless, Arab rejection and the accompanying military conflict led to the foundation of the state of Israel in 1948, which in turn triggered waves of refugee relocation and wars between Israel and the Arab world. In 1967, Israel occupied the West Bank, Gaza Strip, Sinai Peninsula, and Golan Heights during the Six-Day War, which was one of the crucial events that highlighted the conflict.

Other significant occurrences include the Golan Heights and the Sinai Peninsula. Throughout this occupation, tensions have been fueled, and resistance movements, most notably the Palestinian Liberation Organization (PLO) and Hamas, have emerged. The Oslo Accords, which were signed in the 1990s, were an example of peace initiatives that intended to establish a framework for Palestinian self-governance. However, these attempts have been met with obstacles, including the continuous development of settlements and violence.

The war stems from opposing national aspirations, historical grudges, and geographical conflicts. The Israelis place a greater emphasis on security issues and the right to exist as a Jewish-majority state. In contrast, the Palestinians are seeking self-determination and the establishment of an independent state with East Jerusalem as its capital. There are still many controversial issues, including the status of Jerusalem, borders, refugees, and settlements, which are made worse by the presence of religious, cultural, and economic concerns.

It is necessary to resolve fundamental grievances and create confidence between the various parties involved to achieve a peace that will last. This includes respecting the rights and aspirations of both Israelis and Palestinians, settling territorial disputes through discussions based on international law and applicable United Nations resolutions, and encouraging mutual understanding and collaboration between the two groups. Facilitating a debate, providing economic support, and promoting reconciliation initiatives are all areas in which regional and international actors play a significant role.

Israel vs Palestine Conflict Triggering Events

There were weeks of escalating tensions and violence in Jerusalem before the escalation that occurred in May 2021 and October,7,2023. This was especially true in the vicinity of the Al-Aqsa Mosque compound, which is considered a holy place for both Jews and Muslims. Disputes between Palestinians and Israeli security forces broke out as a result of Palestinian demonstrations over the expulsion of Palestinian families from the Sheikh Jarrah area and Israeli police measures at the mosque. These events contributed to the intensification of nationalist emotions on both sides, which in turn contributed to the outbreak of violence.

At the beginning of the year 2022, a series of attacks were carried out in Israel by militants belonging to the Palestinian Islamic Jihad (PIJ) and new, localized groups in the West Bank, which is a territory located northeast of the Gaza Strip and is likewise predominantly inhabited by Palestinians. Since the end of the second Palestinian intifada (uprising; 2000–2005), the Israeli Defense Forces (IDF) retaliated with a series of raids in the West Bank, which resulted in the West Bank experiencing the deadliest year as a result of these raids. However, the Israeli Defense Forces (IDF) did not strike Hamas fighters in the Gaza Strip. Hamas, on the other hand, abstained from intensifying the confrontation, which provided Israeli leaders with additional evidence to support their premise that they could prioritize other dangers over Hamas.

Benjamin Netanyahu returned to his position as Prime Minister of Israel at the end of 2022. He had previously assembled the most far-right cabinet since Israel's independence, which ultimately resulted in a politically unstable government. The government advocated for changes to Israel's fundamental laws that would bring the judicial system under the supervision of the legislature. This controversial move resulted in unprecedented strikes and demonstrations by a large number of Israelis, including thousands of army reservists, who were concerned about the separation of powers. Several senior military officers sent a warning to parliamentarians in August 2023, stating that the Israeli Defense Forces' readiness for war had begun to deteriorate. Provocations made by Hezbollah were increasing the likelihood of a confrontation occurring along Israel's northern border throughout the entire time.

For a long time, Saudi Arabia had conditioned its diplomatic relations with Israel on the successful conclusion of the Israeli-Palestinian peace process. However, at the same time that tensions were rising within the country, Saudi Arabia had launched negotiations with Israel and the United States on a peace treaty between Israel and Saudi Arabia. The Palestinians were not directly involved in the discussions, and it was not anticipated that the arrangement would solve the grievances of the Palestinians in the Israeli-Palestinian conflict. Saudi Arabia did, however, seek concessions on topics that were relevant to the Palestinians. Several experts thought that one of the objectives of

Hamas' attack on October 7 was to impede the discussions that were taking place.

This transaction was a component of a more comprehensive regional restructuring, with the hope that an agreement between Israel and Saudi Arabia would lower the number of resources that the United States needed to dedicate to the Middle East, the United States, which had been the main force behind the peace process for a long time, aimed to make a "pivot to Asia" in its foreign policy initiatives. During this time, Iran was working to strengthen what it called an "axis of resistance" in the area. This "axis of resistance" included Hezbollah in Lebanon, President Bashar al-Assad in Syria, and Houthi opposition in Yemen. Hamas, whose connection with Iran had been turbulent in the 2010s, had grown closer to Iran after 2017 and received significant Iranian backing to build up its military capacity and capability. At the same time, Hamas' relationship with Iran had become more cooperative.

Escalation of The Main Violence: October 7, 2023, Attack

Hamas was the mastermind of a magnificently planned attack that took place on Shemini Atzeret, a Jewish holiday that marks the conclusion of the autumn Thanksgiving feast of Sukkot. This attack took place on October 7, 2023. There were a lot of Israeli Defense Forces soldiers on leave, and the Israeli Defense Forces had been concentrating their attention on the northern border of Israel rather than on the Gaza Strip in the south.

In barely twenty minutes, a barrage of at least 2,200 rockets was launched into Israel, marking the beginning of the assault, which began at approximately 6:30 AM. Throughout that first salvo, Hamas fired more than half of the total amount of rockets that were fired from Gaza over the entire 11-day confrontation that took place in 2021. The Iron Dome system, which is an antimissile defense system that has been deployed throughout Israel and has shown to be highly effective, was overwhelmed by the onslaught; however, the Israeli Defense Force did not indicate how many missiles were able to enter the system. At least 1,500 militants from Hamas and the Palestinian Islamic Jihad (PIJ) infiltrated Israel at dozens of sites using explosives and bulldozers to breach the border, which was extensively defended with sophisticated technology, fencing, and concrete. This occurred while the missiles were raining down on Israel. They damaged the communication networks for several Israeli military positions in the vicinity, which ultimately enabled them to launch attacks against those installations and sneak into civilian districts without being discovered. In the area of the seaside village of Zikim, militants simultaneously breached the maritime boundary using a speedboat. Several individuals entered Israel using motorized paragliders.

The incident resulted in the deaths of around 1,200 individuals, including members of families who were attacked in their homes in kibbutzim, as well as people who were attending an outdoor music festival. Although the majority of them in that number were Israeli civilians, there were also those from other countries. The fact that it was the day that accounted for the most significant number of deaths among Jews since the Holocaust added to the anguish. In addition, some 240 more people were grabbed as captives and brought into the Gaza Strip. At least some of them were seized from the music event, while others were taken from their houses. More than half of the individuals who were taken hostage, including Israelis who claimed dual citizenship, combined carried passports from almost twenty-dozen nations. This effectively pulled other countries into the campaign to liberate their citizens.

At 8:23 in the morning on October 7, the Israeli Defense Force (IDF) declared a state of war readiness and started mobilizing its army reserves. Over the subsequent few days, they eventually called up more than 350,000 reservists. After a delay of two hours, Israeli Defense Force fighter jets started carrying out air strikes in the Gaza Strip. On October 8, Israel proclaimed that it was in a state of war, and Netanyahu instructed the people living in the enclave that was under blockade to be evacuated immediately. We will be everywhere, to the fullest extent of our power. The Israeli government issued an order on October 9 to impose a "complete siege" on the Gaza Strip, which meant that water, energy, food, and gasoline were not allowed to enter the region.

During the time that Israel was carrying out air strikes, international efforts were underway to ensure that the hostages were freed. Qatar, which in previous years had cooperated with Israel on the delivery of foreign humanitarian packages to the Gaza Strip, became the primary mediator; nevertheless, in the first weeks of the war, it was only able to negotiate the release of four of the persons who Hamas was holding. The underground tunnels of Gaza, which formed an intricate web of passageways that extended hundreds of miles, added to the difficulty of locating the hostages as well as targeting militants and their weapons caches. It was difficult to destroy the tunnels without incurring a high civilian cost, and conducting military activity inside the tunnels presented an increased risk for all those who were inside, mainly the Israeli Defense Forces troops and the hostages who might be held there. Within just three weeks of Hamas's attack on October 7, more than 1.4 million Palestinians in the Gaza Strip had been displaced within their own country.

Furthermore, the number of Palestinians who had been killed was still climbing by the thousands, making this conflict the deadliest conflict for Palestinians since the Arab-Israeli war of 1948.

The Israeli ground forces made their way into the Gaza Strip toward the end of October 2010. At first, communications within the zone were cut off, which hindered the militants' capacity to coordinate their actions and made it more difficult for emergency medical services and humanitarian organizations to respond to situations that arose. The ground invasion was relatively slow compared to earlier conflicts, and the number of armored vehicles and people progressively expanded throughout the conflict. For the first time since October 7, the Rafah border crossing between the Gaza Strip and Egypt was opened on November 1. The parameters that Egypt, Hamas, and Israel agreed upon allowed for a limited number of foreign nationals to escape the enclave. This was the first situation that had occurred since October 7.

An agreement was reached on November 22 between the Israeli security cabinet and Hamas on the exchange of prisoners. Qatar and Egypt negotiated the deal, which would coincide with a temporary respite in the hostilities. During the seven-day pause, 110 of the hostages were released in exchange for 240 Palestinian inmates. This was done in exchange for other prisoners. Khan Younis is the central urban hub in the southern part of the Gaza Strip. It is also the location of the homes of crucial Hamas officials, such as Yahya Sinwar and Mohammed Deif. Israeli soldiers went into Khan Younis in the days that followed the resumption of fighting by the Palestinian Authority.

After the year, Israel was under a significant amount of criticism from the international community due to the high number of civilian casualties and widespread destruction in the Gaza Strip. During a fundraiser event for his re-election campaign, Vice President Joe Biden of the United States stated that Israel was beginning to lose support from the international community in the middle of December. At the beginning of January 2024, Israel announced a shift in policy that would result in a more targeted approach. This was in response to the fact that approximately 23,000 Palestinians had been reported dead, the majority of them were civilians but also Hamas fighters. Even though the number of average daily deaths had decreased by one-third since October, it was still more than three times higher than the number of deaths that occurred during the conflict in 2014, which was the deadliest conflict in the Gaza Strip until 2023.

Late in January, a framework was developed between Qatar, Egypt, and the United States for a potential three-phase pause in hostilities, during which a comprehensive agreement to end the war would be discussed. This framework was a result of mediation between these three countries. The pause would entail the release of Palestinian prisoners and hostages whom Israel has detained since the beginning of the conflict. The release would take place in stages from the start of the pause.

Even though the Gaza Strip appeared to be the primary focal point of the conflict, it was not limited to that particular region. Several urban centers in the West Bank were blocked off by the Israeli Defense Forces (IDF), which also increased the frequency of its raids in the region. In October, the IDF carried out an attack by a warplane in the territory for the first time since the second intifada (2000–2005). As Israeli settlers became more watchful, they upped their attacks on Palestinians. Conflicts with Hezbollah in the vicinity of the border with Lebanon posed a risk of opening a second central front, even though both the Israeli Defense Forces and Hezbollah looked reluctant to expand the battle. Attempts by Houthi troops to strike southern Israel, which is an unusual target for the movement based in Yemen, using both missiles and drones also suggested that there was some coordination within the "axis of resistance" led by Iran during the conflict.

Iran's backing of Hamas

The basis for Iran's backing of Hamas, the Palestinian extremist organization, lies in intricate geopolitical, ideological, and strategic factors. To comprehend the reasons for Iran's backing of Hamas, one must examine the historical backdrop of Iran's external strategy, its aspirations in the region, and its position on the Israeli-Palestinian issue. Moreover, assessing the influence of economic aid on Iran's economy necessitates scrutinizing the monetary expenses and diplomatic consequences of such support.

What is the reason behind Iran's support for Hamas?

1 •Geopolitical Factors:

Iran's backing of Hamas is a component of its more comprehensive plan to contest Israel's supremacy in the Middle East and establish its authority in the area. Iran considers Israel as its primary foe and provides support to Palestinian resistance factions, such as Hamas, to offset Israeli influence. Iran supports Hamas to undermine Israel's stance and enhance its leverage in the Arab-Israeli conflict.

2 •Ideological Alignment:

The Islamic revolutionary doctrine of Iran places great importance on demonstrating sympathy with Muslim populations who are oppressed, such as the Palestinians. Iran's support for Hamas is consistent with its ideological dedication to opposing imperialism, Zionism, and perceived Western control in the area. Iran's leadership supports Hamas not just as a strategic decision but also as an expression of its revolutionary ideals and dedication to assisting other Muslims in their fight against perceived injustices.

3 •Proxy warfare:

Iran utilizes proxy organizations such as Hamas as a component of its asymmetric warfare strategy to extend its authority and exert influence in the Middle East. Through its support of Hamas, Iran can indirectly challenge Israel and its supporters without engaging in direct armed conflict. By employing this strategy, Iran can progress toward its strategic goals while ensuring plausible deniability and minimizing the likelihood of direct reprisals.

4 •Israel's deterrence:

Iran views Hamas as a means of deterring Israeli invasion. Iran's objective in providing weapons and assistance to Hamas is to increase the expenses associated with any prospective military intervention by Israel against Iran or its supporters. Hamas's potential for launching strikes against Israel gives Tehran a strategic advantage in regional dynamics and adds complexity to Israel's strategic decision-making process.

5 •Geographical Factors:

Iran's backing of Hamas is also intertwined with its broader regional aspirations and conflicts. Iran aims to counter the dominance of Sunni Arab nations, namely Saudi Arabia, in the Middle East. By providing support to Hamas, Iran can strengthen its connections with Palestinian factions and exert influence over Sunni Arab adversaries, who tend to back more moderate Palestinian factions.

The Economic Consequences of Backing Hamas:

i.Monetary expenses:

Iran's backing of Hamas results in substantial financial expenditures, encompassing monetary assistance, weaponry, training, and logistical support. These expenses redirect resources that could be assigned to domestic priorities, such as infrastructure building, social welfare programs, or economic reforms. Iran's already beleaguered economy is further strained by the financial responsibility of supporting Hamas, which is compounded by international sanctions and economic mismanagement.

ii. Diplomatic Consequences:

Iran's support for Hamas creates complexities in its relationships with other nations, especially those who are associated with Israel or hostile to Hamas' operations. The support that Iran provides to Hamas exacerbates its international isolation and further strains its relationships with countries such as the United governments, Israel, and certain Sunni Arab governments. The isolation of Iran restricts its ability to engage with international markets, attract foreign investment, and pursue diplomatic opportunities, thus impeding its economic prospects.

iii. Effects on Trade and Investment:

Iran's endorsement of Hamas could discourage foreign investment and trade prospects since potential investors and trading partners may be hesitant to deal with a nation seen as a promoter of terrorism. The relationship between Iran and Hamas can have a detrimental impact on efforts to attract foreign investment and technology necessary for economic growth, leading to reputational harm. Furthermore, the imposition of sanctions on Iran as a result of its backing of Hamas can additionally curtail its ability to engage in international markets and hinder its economic expansion.

iv. Humanitarian Expenses:

The allocation of money to aid Hamas detracts from the ability to address urgent humanitarian needs within Iran. As the economic situation worsens, regular Iranians may face limited access to vital services, heightened poverty, and decreased living standards. Allocating funds to militant organizations such as Hamas instead of domestic welfare programs can worsen social disparities and intensify public dissatisfaction with the government.

v. Geopolitical Turmoil:

The assistance provided by Iran to Hamas adds to the instability in the region, intensifying the already high levels of tension in the volatile Middle East. The escalation of conflict between Hamas and Israel can have far-reaching consequences across the region, including energy markets, trade routes, and geopolitical dynamics. The ongoing Israeli-Palestinian conflict, which is partly fueled by Iran's backing of Hamas, extends regional instability and hampers the chances of achieving peace and stability.

Iran's backing of Hamas is motivated by a confluence of geopolitical, ideological, and strategic considerations. Supporting Hamas enables Iran to contest Israel's supremacy in the Middle East and establish its sway in the area. However, this action also entails substantial fiscal burdens and diplomatic obstacles. The financial responsibility of providing support to Hamas redirects resources away from tackling domestic issues, intensifies Iran's economic difficulties, and further isolates it within the international community. Furthermore, Iran's backing of Hamas contributes to the ongoing regional instability, which in turn hampers the chances of achieving peace and prosperity in the Middle East.

Responses And International Involvement to The Israel and Hamas:

Numerous governments, including those of India, Japan, and South Korea, as well as the governments of several Western nations, have condemned the attack that Hamas carried out on October 7. This attack has been blamed for its terroristic behavior against people and has garnered broad criticism from all around the world. Some foreign ministries, particularly those of numerous Arab countries as well as Turkey, Russia, and China, refrained from openly denouncing Hamas and instead advocated moderation. This was especially seen in the case of the Turkish government. Joe Biden, made history on October 18 by becoming the first president of the United States to visit Israel while the country was engaged in a protracted conflict.

Nevertheless, as the conflict caused the humanitarian crisis in the Gaza Strip to worsen, Israel was subjected to a large amount of pressure from the international community to permit a limited amount of aid to enter the region. As the conflict expanded to the southern portion of the Gaza Strip, several individuals who were opposed to the war made allegations of genocide against Israel. In December 2023, South Africa made a request to the International Court of Justice for an injunction to avoid violations of international genocide protocols. Throughout the month that followed, the court issued an injunction mandating that Israel take all possible precautions to prevent genocide, including making it possible for humanitarian aid to be provided throughout the whole Gaza Strip. Concerns were also raised regarding the possibility that the war could escalate into more extensive regional warfare. This is especially true in light of the fact that attacks carried out by Houthi fighters on ships traveling through the Red Sea caused disruptions to global shipping and that U.S. troops stationed in the vicinity were subjected to strikes that may have resulted in fatalities.

There was a surge of anti-Semitism, Islamophobia, anti-Arab, and anti-Palestinian racism as a result of the heated emotions that surrounded the war. There were 312 anti-Semitic events reported in the United States during the first few weeks of the conflict, according to the Anti-Defamation League (ADL). This is an increase over the 64 instances reported during the same period in 2022 (19). During the same period, the Council on American-Islamic Relations (CAIR) received 774 reports of Islamophobia in the United States. This is an increase from the 63 total occurrences reported in August.

In conclusion, the current escalation of the war between Israel and Hamas highlights the urgent need for a comprehensive and long-term resolution to the conflict between Israel and Palestine. To achieve long-term peace and stability in the region, it is vital to address the underlying reasons for the conflict, which include issues with land, security, and the rights of both Israelis and Palestinians. About this undertaking, it is still essential for international efforts to be made to encourage dialogue, reconciliation, and respect for international law.

Effects Of Israel-Hamas War

The Middle East will be the region that will experience the most direct impacts. Benjamin Netanyahu, the Prime Minister of Israel, has been operating under delusions for many years, but those illusions have now been destroyed. The anticipation that Israel might normalize its relations with the Arab world without addressing the Palestinian question, which he apparently believed could be wished away, was the most significant of these expectations from his perspective.

These days, it is impossible to disregard the subject that has been raised. Regardless of the results of its attack in Gaza, Israel will have to engage in some weighty introspection, and it may have to completely reevaluate its approach to the stagnant peace process in the Middle East altogether. It is highly likely that Saudi Arabia, which was on the verge of normalizing relations with Israel, will now demand certain concessions for the Palestinians before moving forward. This is because Saudi Arabia wishes to avoid incurring the ire of its populace as well as the rest of the Muslim world.

Without a shadow of a doubt, Israel possesses the right to defend itself. However, Netanyahu may prolong the conflict or encourage a regional escalation to recover control of the story and maintain his political position. Netanyahu may be expecting to restore his ideal geopolitical constellation, which is Israel and the Sunni Arab states facing off against Iran's 'axis of resistance.' The Palestinians are once again reduced to a sideshow in a far larger clash. This is because Netanyahu's putative friends in the Gulf are on the fence.

In addition, the crisis will have severe repercussions outside the Middle East, with Ukraine being one of the countries that would suffer the most. The acts of violence and misery that the people of this country are currently experiencing do not appear to be nearly as extraordinary as they were in the past. As heartbreaking as everything that has come out of Kharkiv or Mariupol, the images that are being relayed from Gaza are particularly severe. Moreover, the battle in Gaza gives the impression to many people that the situation in Ukraine is a "local" European conflict.

As a result of the fact that the continuous support of the international community is essential to the survival of Ukraine, anything that diverts attention away from its struggle is unfavorable news. Furthermore, if the conflict between Israel and Hamas worsens, with Iran joining the fray, the impact on oil prices could make it more expensive for the West to continue its restrictions on Russian energy.

Several difficulties are brought to the attention of Europe as a whole by the catastrophe in Gaza. First, it has brought to light significant fault lines within France, Germany, and the United Kingdom. To give just one example, France has reported a more substantial number of antisemitic events in the past three weeks than it had in the entire previous year. Concurrently, the conflict between Israel and Hamas has contributed to the fracturing of other member states of the European Union.

In the aftermath of Russia's full-scale invasion of Ukraine in the previous year, European nations have shown an extraordinary level of togetherness. However, the leaders of the European Union are currently dividing their attention between Gaza, Ukraine, and Nagorno-Karabakh, which Azerbaijan recently regained following a military attack that lasted for twenty-four hours. The resolution that calls for a humanitarian truce in Gaza was put to a vote by the United Nations General Assembly on October 27. The member states of the European Union voted in three distinct ways.

Due to the shambolic response of the European Union (EU) to the war between Israel and Hamas, China's robust reaction has become even more noticeable. On the other hand, China promptly proclaimed its support for the Palestinians, in contrast to its efforts to maintain its neutrality during Russia's invasion of Ukraine. China has incorporated its reaction as part of its outreach to countries in the global south. And there is little doubt that Chinese officials are eagerly anticipating the opportunity to bring attention to the Western world's double standards, which include Israel's opposition to Russia and the Palestinians' opposition to the Ukrainians, in the weeks and months ahead.

If China were to choose a side, however, it may result in issues. A more widespread conflict in the region could destabilize the fragile truce China has managed to broker between Saudi Arabia and Iran. As for the United States of America, it has become a cliche to explain its experience in the Middle East by referring to a line from The Godfather Part III: "Just when I thought I was out, they pull me back in!" Because the government of Vice President Joe Biden of the United States has demonstrated a significantly higher level of discipline and commitment in promoting a foreign policy pivot from the Middle East to Asia than either of his immediate predecessors, Barack Obama and Donald Trump; this is particularly pertinent in the present day. But now, the area is again at the top of the agenda for policymakers in the United States.

As of this moment, Vice President Biden has done an excellent job of striking a balance between his support for Israel and his demands for the Israelis to respond to the attack by Hamas with more remarkable restraint. In addition, his choice to include support for Israel and help for Ukraine in a single national security package presents an opportunity to be successful in overcoming opposition from Republican members who are opposed to assisting Ukraine.

Despite this, Biden is striding precariously on a tightrope. At that point, Ukraine was already an undesirable distraction from the most important thing for the United States of America, which was the strategic battle with China. Considering this, the United States of America does not require any more involvement in the Middle East.

It is pretty unlikely that anyone, with the possible exception of Hamas and Netanyahu, would be interested in prolonging or expanding the conflict that is currently taking place in Gaza. Possibly against one's better judgment, one hopes the relevant parties will acknowledge their common interests and collaborate to achieve them. This ensures that the disagreement is resolved as fast as possible, without any further escalation, which is of the utmost importance. After the military component of Hamas has been decimated and its Israeli prisoners have been released, it means moving forward with efforts to find a political solution to the conflict between Israel and the Palestinians. Israel's long-term security cannot be ensured in any other way than through this method.

International Efforts Towards Peace and Resolution of Israel and Hamas War

a) Possible New U.S. Sales of Combat Aircraft to Israel

Sources revealed in January 2024 that the United States and Israel are concluding up to three different sales of fixed-wing aircraft (25 F-35Is and 25 F-15IAs) and rotary-wing aircraft (12 Apache helicopters) to Israel. These transactions are expected to be finalized shortly. In addition, reports indicate that Israel has been "accelerating acquisition of various kinds of aerial munitions," which are estimated to be worth "hundreds of millions of dollars." This is even though delivering such products is expected to take years.

b) Humanitarian Assistance for Palestinians

For "helping support over a million displaced and conflict-affected people with clean water, food, hygiene support, medical care, and other essential needs," President Biden recently announced that the United States will provide $100 million in humanitarian assistance to Gaza and the West Bank during his visit to Israel on October 18. This assistance will be provided through "trusted partners, including United Nations agencies and international non-governmental organizations." According to the United States Agency for International Development (USAID), as of the middle of January, the Bureau of Humanitarian Assistance of USAID had committed $43.3 million in assistance for Gaza and the West Bank for the fiscal year 2024.

Additionally, the Bureau of Population, Refugees, and Migration of the Department of State had committed $51 million for Gaza and the West Bank through the United Nations Relief and Works Agency for Palestine Refugees in the Near East (UNRWA) and $18.2 million for the region through another implementing partner. Due to claims that twelve employees of the United Nations Relief and Works Agency (UNRWA) were involved in the attacks on October 7, the United States Department of State has declared that it will temporarily freeze UNRWA's unobligated funding. Several lawmakers have sponsored legislation or sent letters that demand a halt to humanitarian help in Gaza and more excellent monitoring of whether or not any assistance from the United States to Gaza and the West Bank may have been diverted in the past or may be at risk of being delayed in the future by Hamas or other parties. There have been 58 other lawmakers who have advocated for the Palestinians to get extra humanitarian assistance. In addition, legislators are discussing the extent to which the United Nations Relief and Works Agency (UNRWA) or other implementing partners might provide humanitarian aid while minimizing the dangers of wrongdoing.

c) The Legislation Concerning Supplemental Appropriations

Vice President Joe Biden announced in a speech in the Oval Office on October 19 that he would request an emergency supplemental budget to support the United States partners, such as Ukraine, Israel, and others, and address other domestic and global challenges. The President is requesting more than $14 billion in funding for Israel-related projects. Over more than three months, the House of Representatives and the Senate have been deliberating on their different versions of supplemental appropriations legislation. These bills have not only been focused on Israel but also on other domestic and foreign policy issues, such as providing help to Ukraine and Taiwan and altering the laws regarding the United States' borders and taxes. The House of Representatives and the Senate announced that they had changed their supplemental appropriations legislation at the beginning of February 2024. On February 3, House leaders released a base text (H.R. 7217), which would provide the total amount requested by the President (with additional defense funds for artillery and munitions) while adding $2.5 billion in FY2024 Presidential Drawdown Authority (22 U.S.C. 2318(a)(1)) for Israel, which "shall not take effect" unless the Secretary of State determines and reports to Congress that the exercise of such authority is in response to the situation in Israel.

Additionally, the measure would allocate $3.3 billion in defense expenditures to the Department of Defense (D.O.D.) to support ongoing operations in the area of operations maintained by the United States Central Command (CENTCOM). The stand-alone Israel aid bill has been threatened with a veto by President Biden, who has stated so. The leaders of the Senate proposed a revised bill the next day (the original Senate supplemental had been introduced in early December as S.Amdt. 1371 to H.R.815) that appropriated a total of $118.3 billion for various domestic and international challenges.

d) The United States may provide Israel with additional assistance

The United States government may be considering whether to enhance, maintain, decrease, or condition the current level of support it provides to Israel. S.Res, 504, a privileged resolution, was introduced by Senator Bernie Sanders in December 2023. The resolution would have mandated that the State Department provide Congress with information on Israel's human rights practices within thirty days of its passage by Section 502B(c) of the Foreign Assistance Act 1961. Following receipt of the report, Congress may take action to cancel, restrict, or continue providing security aid to Israel through a joint resolution. The Senate approved a motion to remove Senate Resolution 504 from the jurisdiction of the Senate Foreign Relations Committee on January 16, 2024, with a vote in favor of 72-11. According to a story that the White House has refuted,70 it has been indicated that the White House is contemplating the possibility of reducing or pausing the delivery of munitions from the United States to Israel as a means of gaining agreement on specific requests made by the United States, such as the cooperation of Israel in giving additional assistance to Palestinian civilians.

e) The Monitoring of United States Security Assistance for Human Rights

Since the Israeli Defense Forces (I.D.F.) began its operations in Gaza, there have been allegations that Israel has caused an excessive number of civilian casualties and may have misused defense equipment from the United States. Additionally, officials from the Biden administration have become more vociferous in their demand that Israel pay attention to civilian losses. Israel is reportedly taking measures to limit the number of civilian casualties, according to statements made by officials from the United States. "They have [the Israelis] relied less on-air power, structured their ground operations in such a way, to try to be more targeted and precise," said John Kirby, who is the spokesperson for the White House's National Security Council. I am constantly told that they are choosing to ignore us and that they are not paying attention to what we have to say, but the truth is that the facts do not support this assertion. There is a report that states that the United States of America and Israel have established a bilateral channel to evaluate complaints of civilian injury, stating that The Biden administration is reportedly delaying the delivery of 27,000 M4 and M16 rifles to Israel's national police due to concerns that such armaments may be transferred to civilians under an initiative led by Israel's ultra-nationalist National

Security Minister Itamar Ben Gvir. This information was reported in a report that was published in the middle of December.

Chapter 3: China's Ascendancy: Regional Ambitions and Global Impact

China's prominence signifies a substantial shift in the global balance of power and has repercussions for geopolitics, economics, and international relations. The rise of China has resulted in several disagreements about international relations. These disagreements are a consequence of alterations in the global balance of power and China's forceful activities in pursuing its objectives. Disagreements and tensions that have arisen as a direct result of China's rise to power are as follows.

1. South China Sea territorial disputes

The South China Sea is at the epicentre of one of the most controversial and complicated territorial disputes that the globe is currently facing during this period. In addition to being abundant in natural riches and key maritime lanes, this region is also strategically important. It is of immense geopolitical significance. It is possible to trace the origins of the dispute over the South China Sea back hundreds of years because several historical records indicate that multiple nations in the region engaged in fishing and commerce activities. On the other hand, contemporary territorial claims frequently depend on past narratives, particularly China's declaration of sovereignty, which is based on historical records and ancient maps. The so-called "Nine-Dash Line," which spans approximately 90 percent of the South China Sea, is the boundary from which China asserts its claim to almost the entire South China Sea.

Key Players and Territorial Claims: China:

To strengthen its presence in the South China Sea, China has taken a proactive approach to its claims, which includes reclaiming land and constructing artificial islands. China also says that it has historical rights over the region. The expansive allegations that it has made overlap with those of other claimants have caused great worry among the countries near it and the international community.

Vietnam:

There are historical connections between Vietnam and the Paracel and Spratly Islands, and Vietnam asserts its sovereignty over several features in the South China Sea. To maintain its claims, it has engaged in diplomatic and legal initiatives and vigorously challenged China's assertiveness.

Philippines:

Certain features in the South China Sea, such as the Scarborough Shoal and portions of the Spratly Islands, are contested by the Philippines, which asserts its sovereignty over these features. An international tribunal favoured the Philippines in 2016 invalidated China's historical claims and argued that specific characteristics did not have the right to exclusive economic zones (EEZs) or continental shelves.

Malaysia:

According to the United Nations Convention on the Law of the Sea (UNCLOS), Malaysia asserts its control over marine zones. It claims a portion of the Spratly Islands as its territory. It has voiced concerns regarding China's aggressive operations in the geographical area.

Brunei:

Because Brunei has a relatively short coastline along the South China Sea, it has not been as actively involved in the territorial disputes as other claims have been. This organization advocates for a peaceful resolution that is founded on international law.

Taiwan:

Based on historical claims, Taiwan, much like China, proclaims its sovereignty over the entirety of the South China Sea. However, Taiwan's government retains a sizeable military presence in the region despite having limited international recognition.

Legislative Structure:

The United Nations Convention on the Law of the Sea (UNCLOS) is the primary source of the legal framework governing the South China Sea dispute. This convention was created to give principles for the delimitation of maritime boundaries, the establishment of exclusive economic zones (EEZs), and the rights of coastal governments. Certain legal aspects of the issue were clarified as a result of the decision made by the tribunal in the case that the Philippines brought against China. These aspects included the status of certain maritime features and the rights of coastal nations.

Perspectives on Recent Events and Their Implications:

The South China Sea continues to be a hotbed of geopolitical competition and maritime brinkmanship despite the extensive efforts that the international community has made to moderate tensions and encourage peaceful resolution. Concerns have been voiced over freedom of navigation, regional stability, and the potential for conflict escalation as a result of China's ongoing fortification of artificial islands, construction operations, and assertive maritime patrols.

In addition to having far-reaching ramifications for regional security and economic interests, the dispute over the South China Sea also has implications for the rules-based international order. As a result, claimant governments have boosted their spending on defence, enlarged their military deployments, and improved their level of security cooperation with foreign entities such as the United governments of America, Japan, and Australia. Furthermore, the disagreement has strained diplomatic relations, hampered measures to promote regional cooperation, and inflamed nationalist sentiments among the populations of countries that have been affected.

Efforts made to manage the conflict in the South China Sea using diplomatic means, such as multilateral consultations and steps to create confidence, have been met with substantial hurdles. Despite considerable progress in implementing a legally binding code of behaviour between claimant states, differences continue to exist over essential issues such as territorial claims, the exploitation of resources, and the processes for conflict resolution.

According to the territorial disputes in the South China Sea represent a complex and dangerous flashpoint in international relations. These disputes are characterized by opposing territory claims, historical grudges, and geopolitical rivalry. If the dispute is to be effectively managed, it is necessary to maintain diplomatic engagement, respect international law, and commit to finding a peaceful resolution. Failure to do so could result in the region devolving into violence, which would have far-reaching ramifications for the security and economy of the entire world.

Analysis Of China's Increasing Assertiveness in The Asia-Pacific Region

In the past few years, China's increasing assertiveness in the Asia-Pacific area has emerged as a critical geopolitical phenomenon that has far-reaching repercussions for the region's stability and international relations. Various elements, such as China's economic and military rise, nationalist narratives, and geopolitical ambitions, drive this assertiveness.

China has become the preeminent economic force in the region due to its rapid economic growth, which has provided it with the resources and influence necessary to accomplish its strategic objectives. China can project force and assert its territorial claims in the South China Sea and East China Sea due to its enormous investments in military modernization, which complements the country's economic strength.

China's forceful behaviour is frequently placed within nationalist narratives that portray China as regaining lost areas and striving to establish itself as a regional hegemon. These narratives provide a framework for China's behaviour. The Chinese Communist Party (CCP) uses historical grievances to legitimize its activities, which in turn helps cultivate a sense of national pride and solidarity among the Chinese people.

China's assertiveness can be seen in several ways, including territorial disputes, military posturing, and diplomatic pressure. To strengthen its position in the South China Sea, China has reclaimed land, erected artificial islands, and deployed military equipment. This has increased tensions with the countries that are located near China as well as with the United States. In addition, China has engaged in provocative military manoeuvres, declared air defence identification zones (ADIZs), and utilized coercive economic measures to exert pressure on countries in the region to align themselves with China's objectives.

Countries in the region have responded to China's aggressiveness in various ways, with some attempting to strike a balance between engaging with China and protecting themselves from its expanding influence. Because of this, stronger security links have been established, closer alliances have been formed with the United States, and efforts have been made to maintain a rules-based order in the region. On the other hand, countries' vulnerabilities have been established due to their economic dependence on China, which has made it more difficult for them to push back against China's aggression. China's growing assertiveness has significant repercussions, including an increase in the likelihood of conflict and instability in the Asia-Pacific area. The intensification of military tensions, the ongoing weapons race, and the possibility of maritime incidents substantially concern the region's security. Furthermore, the assertive behaviour of China undermines the international order founded on rules and threatens to restructure the region's dynamics in accordance with China's own interests.

A multidimensional approach that combines diplomatic engagement, multilateral collaboration, and commitment to international law and standards is required to address the problems posed by China's assertiveness. The concepts of transparency, dialogue, and respect for sovereignty must serve as the guiding principles for your efforts to manage tensions and maintain regional stability. Only through concerted efforts to address the underlying drivers of conflict can the Asia-Pacific region manage the complexity of China's increasing assertiveness and construct a safer and prosperous future for all stakeholders involved.

2. The Trade Disputes Between China and The United States

Trade conflicts between China and the United States have become a defining characteristic of global economic relations. These disagreements are fueled by China's rising assertiveness and the United States' worries over unfair trade practices and strategic competition. However, China has become more assertive in recent years. These disagreements have significant repercussions for the dynamics of the world economy, geopolitics, and the course that international relations will take. The continuous trade conflicts between China and the United States are causing widespread worldwide unrest. These issues have a wide-ranging influence on economies, businesses, and international relations. The ripple effects of these conflicts, characterized by growing tariffs, retaliatory measures, and increased uncertainty, extend far beyond the two countries directly involved in the dispute. This is how these trade disputes are adding to the upheaval that is occurring all across the world:

1. 4Economic Disruption:

As a result of the trade disputes between China and the United States, global supply chains and trade flows have been disrupted, which has resulted in more excellent prices for businesses, decreased consumer spending, and increased market volatility. Investment and economic growth have been hampered due to the uncertainty surrounding trade policies and tariffs. This has been the case not just in the two directly involved nations but also in economies worldwide dependent on international commerce.

2. 5Market Volatility:

There has been an increase in market volatility across the world's financial markets due to the uncertainty surrounding trade negotiations and the introduction of tariffs. The fluctuations in the stock markets are a direct result of each new development in the trade conflicts. These fluctuations hurt investor confidence and exacerbate concerns regarding the stability of the global economy.

3. 6Interruptions in the Supply Chain:

Numerous sectors depend on intricate global supply chains in which raw materials and finished goods travel through several countries before being delivered to end users. These supply chains are disrupted due to the implementation of tariffs and trade barriers, which results in delays, increased costs, and inefficiencies in the production processes. Every sector of the economy is impacted by this upheaval, from the manufacturing and technology sectors to the agricultural and automotive sectors.

4. 7Global Growth Concerns:

Concerns about the broader outlook for economic growth worldwide have been expressed as a result of the trade disputes between China and the United States. Because they are two of the most significant economies in the world, interruptions in their trade connection have a considerable impact on what is projected to happen to global GDP growth. There is considerable uncertainty regarding trade policies, in addition to slower development in China and the United States, which weighs significantly on the prognosis for the global economy.

5. 8The Effects of Spillover:

Spillover effects reach beyond the borders of China and the United States due to the bilateral trade issues between the two countries. In addition to the United States and China, other nations, particularly those with close economic relations with either of those two countries, are also impacted by changes in trade policy and market conditions. Due to trade disputes, countries that are highly reliant on exports or susceptible to changes in global trade patterns face difficulties in their economic situations.

6.9Current Geopolitical Tensions:

Existing geopolitical tensions and rivalries are exacerbated by the trade disputes between China and the United States, which contribute to an international environment that is increasingly unclear and unstable. The disagreements are part of a more significant strategic battle between the two countries for influence and domination in various places. This competition further complicates efforts to address other global concerns, such as climate change, security threats, and global health crises.

To summarise, the trade disputes that are taking place between the United States and China are producing considerable global turbulence, which is causing disruptions in the economies, financial markets, supply networks, and geopolitical dynamics. Concerns about the broader prospects for the worldwide economy are raised due to the ambiguity surrounding trade policies and the application of tariffs, both of which contribute to economic instability. Coordinated efforts from all parties concerned will be needed to develop mutually acceptable solutions and respect the ideals of open, fair, and rules- based trade to resolve these issues and restore stability to the global trading system.

3. Taiwan Cross-Strait Relations with China

Over several decades, the relationship between Taiwan and China, generally referred to as Cross-Strait Relations, has been a focal point of geopolitical conflict. The conflict originates from the Chinese Civil War and the partition in 1949 between mainland China, which was headed by the Communist Party, and Taiwan, which was led by the Kuomintang, on the nationalist side. Because of this separation, there have been complicated diplomatic, economic, and security challenges, which have caused waves of unrest all across the world.

This war between Taiwan and China may be traced back to the Chinese Civil War, which led to the retreat of Kuomintang forces to Taiwan and the foundation of the People's Republic of China (PRC) on the mainland. The dispute between Taiwan and China has its origins in this conflict. Since then, both sides have asserted their sovereignty over the entirety of China, and neither side has acknowledged the authority of the other. Despite this, Taiwan has evolved into a prosperous democracy with a distinct political and cultural identity different from mainland China's.

Conflicts between Taiwan and China have been more intense over the past few years due to several different issues. Concerns have been expressed worldwide due to China's growing assertiveness in its territorial claims, particularly in the South China Sea. The Chinese capital of Beijing has persistently adopted a policy of diplomatic marginalization of Taiwan, exerting pressure on other nations and international organizations to desist from recognizing or dealing with Taiwan as a sovereign state. The Chinese government has also increased the number of military drills and sabre-rattling exercises, which include frequent violations of Taiwan's airspace and naval manoeuvres near Taiwan.

The confrontation between Taiwan and China has enormous repercussions for the stability and security of the world. In the first place, it makes the geopolitical tensions that already exist in the Asia-Pacific region worse. The United States of America, which is Taiwan's most important friend, has committed to defend Taiwan against any invasion from China. This has raised the possibility of a military clash between the two largest economies in the world. If this scenario were to occur, it would have significant repercussions for international trade, supply chains, and the economy's stability.

The second point is that the struggle between Taiwan and China is intertwined with more giant geopolitical rivalries, particularly between the United States and China. By strengthening its connections with Taiwan and other allies in the Indo-Pacific region, the United States has been working to counteract the growing influence that China is exerting in the area. As a result, there has been an increase in the military presence, sales of armaments, and diplomatic backing for Taiwan, which has further caused tensions with Beijing to escalate.

Thirdly, the conflict between Taiwan and China makes it more difficult for international organizations to address global concerns such as economic development, pandemics, and climate change. The absence of Taiwan from international organizations such as the World Health Organisation (WHO) due to pressure from China has hampered worldwide cooperation in the fight against public health crises, as demonstrated during the COVID-19 pandemic.

Because Taiwan and China are hesitant to make concessions on their territorial claims, the possibility of a conflict between them continues to be a looming danger. Any effort made by Taiwan to declare its legal independence will likely be met with a severe response from

Beijing, which might escalate to a military confrontation. On the other hand, China's persistent efforts to isolate Taiwan diplomatically and militarily could bring Taiwan closer to the point when it seeks formal independence, which would further escalate tensions across the region.

It has been challenging to find a solution to the Taiwan-China dispute because of the entrenched political stances and historical grievances between the two countries. On the other hand, discussion and diplomacy continue to be vital instruments for de-escalation and preventing conflicts. The international community, which includes regional stakeholders and global powers, is obligated to play a positive role in promoting discussion, cultivating mutual trust, and locating peaceful solutions to the problem between Taiwan and China.

In conclusion, the confrontation between Taiwan and China is a massive hotspot in global geopolitics, and it has significantly far-reaching repercussions for the stability of the area, the security of the international community, and the governance of the entire world. Tensions between the two sides continue to be fueled by Taiwan's unsettled status, which exacerbates the existing geopolitical rivalries and makes it more challenging to address global concerns. There is a need for coordinated efforts to engage in discussion, establish trust, and seek peaceful settlements to the disagreement between Taiwan and China. This is necessary to reduce the likelihood of confrontation and to help promote peace and stability.

4. The China's Belt and Road Initiative (BRI) and Its Global Impact

The Belt and Road Initiative (BRI), initiated by China in 2013, is an ambitious initiative that aims to enhance infrastructure and economic development across multiple continents. China aims to improve connectivity along the old Silk Road routes by constructing a network of roads, railroads, ports, and other infrastructure projects. This will allow China to encourage trade and investment along these routes. However, even though the Belt and Road Initiative (BRI) has the potential to bring about considerable economic gains, it has also given rise to concerns and controversies, which have resulted in worldwide conflict.

The Scope and Objectives of the BRI

In addition to encompassing more than sixty percent of the world's population and a sizeable percentage of the global GDP, the Belt and Road Initiative (BRI) spans more than seventy countries, including those in Asia, Africa, Europe, and Oceania. The Belt and Road Initiative (BRI) is comprised of China's core goals: to encourage economic growth, improve regional collaboration, and increase China's influence on the international stage. China's goal is to address internal overcapacity issues and assist the internationalization of its currency, the yuan, through its investment in infrastructure projects that it is doing.

Opportunities and Obstacles of BRI

The Belt and Road Initiative (BRI) offers the potential for developing infrastructure, creating jobs, and greater commerce and investment for the participating nations. Numerous developing countries are pleased to receive Chinese investment since it helps to bridge critical financial shortages for infrastructure projects that are desperately required. On the other hand, concerns have been expressed over the terms of Chinese financing, which frequently involve large amounts of debt and lack transparency. Those opposed to such agreements claim that they could result in a dependency on debt and threaten the sovereignty of the countries receiving the debt.

Geopolitical Implications of BRI

There are considerable geopolitical ramifications associated with the Belt and Road Initiative (BRI), which raises issues about China's expanding power and its strategic goals. Several people believe that China is using this project to broaden its sphere of influence and pose a challenge to the current global order, which is dominated by Western powers. In critical locations, constructing new infrastructure networks and economic corridors can reconfigure trade routes and shift the balance of power in those regions. In addition, the growing presence of China in strategically significant locations, such as ports and naval bases, has stoked concerns regarding the country's aspirations to improve its military capabilities.

Environmental and Social Concerns of BRI

The Belt and Road Initiative's (BRI) focus on infrastructure construction has created environmental and socioeconomic problems. It is possible for large-scale projects, such as dams and highways, to hurt the ecosystems and communities that are located nearby. Critics contend that environmental sustainability and social safeguards need to receive more attention, which has destroyed forests, the relocation of indigenous peoples, and other unfavourable outcomes. Taking action to address these problems is necessary to guarantee BRI projects' long-term profitability and success.

Technological Dominance and Security Risks

Concerns regarding data security and technical dominance have been expressed due to China's participation in creating digital infrastructure as part of the Belt and Road Initiative (BRI). Within the Belt and Road Initiative (BRI), Chinese businesses such as Huawei are significantly involved in constructing 5G networks and supplying telecommunications equipment to countries. Because of this, there are concerns that China would utilize its technology skills for espionage and monitoring, which would increase the security risks for both the participating countries and the international community as a whole.

Responses from the International Community on BRI

The Belt and Road Initiative (BRI) has been met with a range of reactions from the global community. Although some nations have enthusiastically welcomed Chinese investment and involvement in the effort, some nations have voiced misgivings or outright hostility. Some countries have reconsidered their participation in Belt and Road Initiative (BRI) projects due to concerns about the sustainability of their debt, the impact on the environment, and geopolitical motivations. Additionally, the United States of America and other Western powers have expressed concern about the geopolitical repercussions that could result from China's growing influence. These nations have also tried to offset this influence through alternative initiatives, such as the Indo-Pacific strategy.

In conclusion, a bold goal for economic development and connectivity on a global scale is represented by the Belt and Road Initiative (BRI). The Belt and Road Initiative (BRI) presents several substantial hurdles and concerns even though it may provide potential benefits to the nations that participate, such as more significant trade and investments in infrastructure. The programme has caused global unrest and spurred arguments about its implications for the future of international relations. It has caused problems such as dependence on debt, environmental damage, geopolitical conflicts, and dangers to national security. To effectively address these concerns, it will be necessary for all parties involved in the Belt and Road Initiative (BRI) to increase their level of transparency, accountability, and cooperation. In the end, the success of the initiative will be determined by its capacity to generate development outcomes that are both sustainable and inclusive, which will be to the benefit of all parties related to the effort.

Chapter 4: Indian Politics and Economic Outlook

Examination of the political landscape and upcoming elections in India

India is the biggest democracy in the world, a mix of different government systems, cultures, and socioeconomic situations. As the country prepares for the upcoming elections, a close look at its political scene shows a tapestry of complex threads of historical memories, regional dynamics, and modern problems.

The Indian main political parties and coalitions

The Indian political scene is dominated by a few big parties and coalitions:

I. Bharatiya Janata Party (BJP): The BJP has been the most powerful political force in India for the past ten years. It is a right-wing party with strong nationalist and Hindu- centered beliefs. The BJP, led by Prime

Minister Narendra Modi, has made a lot of changes to the economy and society. However, it has also been criticized for policies that people think cause disagreement.

II. Indian National Congress (INC): The INC used to be India's most powerful political party, but its power has been waning in recent years. The Gandhi family runs the party, which supports a secular, open, and welfare-focused approach. However, the party has had problems with leadership and organization.

III. Regional Parties: Also, India's politics are affected by other many regional parties, like the All India Trinamool Congress (TMC) in West Bengal, the Dravida Munnetra Kazhagam (DMK) in Tamil Nadu, and the Telangana Rashtra Samithi (TRS) in Telangana. In their own states, these parties are very important, and they often have an effect on national politics through coalitions and alliances.

In this study, many aspects of Indian politics are examined, using facts and figures to shed light on the current situation and predict the expected global turmoil due to the results of the election.

Historical Background and Changes in Politics

India's political history is full of important events and changes in ideas that have shaped its path. India got its freedom from British colonial rule in 1947. Since then, the Indian National Congress (INC) party has been in charge of politics, and with its commitment to secularism, socialism, and non-alignment, the INC, which was led by famous people like Jawaharlal Nehru and Indira Gandhi, shaped the country's early path after freedom.

However, the political scene changed dramatically when new political parties like the Bharatiya Janata Party (BJP) came into power. The BJP was founded in 1980 with a clear Hindutva (Hindu nationalist) philosophy. It quickly became well-known, challenging the INC's dominance and eventually taking over nationally. When the BJP came to power, especially under Narendra Modi's direction, it started a new era in Indian politics marked by strong nationalism, economic reforms, and cultural conservatism.

The Results of India's Elections and What It Means to The World

In seven stages, 640 million Indians went to the polls to vote in the 2024 Indian general election. It was the biggest election in the history of the country. The lower house of parliament, the Lok Sabha, had elections for all 543 seats. The Bhartiya Janata Party (BJP) and the Indian National Congress (INC), along with their coalitions, were competing for a majority.

People and observers alike had a lot of negative things to say about this important election. This was mostly because of what the BJP and the current Prime Minister Narendra Modi did. There were many complaints about the election, but the results surprised many people who thought the BJP would win by a huge margin, like they did in 2014 and 2019. The BJP and Modi did get a third term, but they did not get enough seats to form a majority. This was the first time they had to form a coalition government.

Indians' Democracy During the June 2024 General Elections

In the last few years, there have been signs that India's democracy is weaker. Today, polls like V-Dem call India an electoral autocracy, which means that the country has free elections but weaker protections for civil rights and freedoms. Those who have been closely monitoring Indian democracy prior to the election have identified three main concerns. First, reporters reported instances of violence, threats, and various forms of voter suppression prior to and during the election. These incidents appeared to target Muslims more than any other group. Worse, reports say that the criminals were sometimes people working for the government, like police officers. Secondly, numerous candidates from various parties withdrew from the race prior to the election. This meant that BJP candidates ran unopposed in a lot of seats. Reports say that police and other state agents have been trying to scare these candidates into dropping out. Thirdly, the Election Commission of India has been involved in some questionable practices. This situation is peculiar as the Election Commission of India is expected to act as a vigilant watchdog. New reports say that the ECI chose not to punish Modi for his hate speech on purpose, especially after his famous speech in Banswara, Rajasthan, where he called Muslim citizens "infiltrators." The ECI did nothing to stop this and other hate speech, which made people seriously question its reputation as an impartial judge. The BJP later lost that seat by a large margin.

The past ten years of BJP rule have steadily eroded India's rights and democratic freedoms. India's government went from being an electoral democracy to an electoral autocracy in 2018, according to the Swedish Varieties of Democracy Institute. In practice, this means that even though there are multiparty elections, basic rights like free speech and fair elections are not well protected. Additionally, the executive has increased its power as it has risen through the ranks. In tandem with these challenges to democratic institutions, the prevalence of Hindu supremacist ethno-majoritarianism has increased. In the past, India regarded this worldview as marginal. As Hindu nationalism has grown, there has been a sharp rise in violent crimes against minorities, especially crimes against India's 200 million Muslims, whom Hindu nationalists see as "infiltrators." These changes are all detrimental for a liberal democracy and a society with many different kinds of people.

Narendra Modi and his BJP party won another term: How did the BJP come to dominate Indian politics?

Yes, they did win another term, but not with nearly as much support as they did in the last two federal elections. The BJP only won 240 seats this time, down from 303 in 2019, which was not enough to have an absolute majority. This means that the BJP won't be able to set the national agenda on its own; instead, it will have to work with smaller parties like the TDP and the JD (U) to make it happen. It will also face much stronger opposition from the Indian National Congress and its coalition partners, known as the "India" block, than was first thought. This means the BJP will have less election control than before. There are many parts to the story of the BJP's rise. One part is the history of the Congress Party's long decline. The Congress Party led India to independence and ran Indian politics for 54 years. This was partly due to the fact that the Congress had failed in both economic and social areas. Another reason was that historically oppressed groups, such as "lower" castes, became more politically active and found a voice outside of the elite-controlled Congress. This started in the 1960s and sped up in the 1970s and 1980s. At the same time, the marginalized castes were facing opposition from upper-caste and upper-class people. After its founding in 1980, the BJP grew in part by capitalizing on this backlash.

Many Indians were shocked by the results of this election. The BJP did not get a majority, and the Prime Minister did not clearly win. Now, to form a government, the BJP requires a large number of minor allies. Many of these allies may not align with all of the BJP's primary policies. In spite of what the exit polls said, the current government did not win by a huge margin. The India bloc, which is opposed to the BJP, got 232 seats, while the NDA alliance bloc got 293 seats. Modi won a third term, but he will now have to deal with coalition politics, which is new for this version of his party (the BJP did not get the 272 seats it needs for a simple majority). Over the last ten years, Modi has become a symbol of the BJP and Indian leadership. This is a huge upset in the election. There's no doubt that the BJP ruled Indian politics for ten years, but it depended a lot on one man and his image. But these results make us question that trust and wonder if he is now a liability or just past his best. Even though the Prime Minister won his constituency (Varanasi), it was by a much smaller margin than in previous years, as well as compared to other prime ministers who ran for parliament while they were in office.

Global Relations with India and What These Election Results Puts at Stake

First, you should know that the BJP is a part of a Hindu supremacist movement that has been going on for almost 100 years. This movement is likely the world's largest neo-fascist movement. Since Modi took power in 2014, that movement has come a long way. The passage of a set of discriminatory citizenship laws, which would connect India's idea of citizenship to religion for the first time, is one of its most important "victories." The Citizenship Amendment Act (CAA), masquerading as persecuted minorities from neighboring countries, expedites the citizenship process for non-Muslim religious minorities. The act explicitly excludes Muslims. The National

Register of Citizens (NRC) aims to eliminate "doubtful citizens." This implies that numerous Muslims and individuals from other impoverished communities, lacking "official" documentation, may face imprisonment or deportation. Civil society's opposition initially put these reforms on hold, but the BJP has now pledged to resume their implementation. For India's minorities, and really for anyone who believes in democracy, there is a lot at stake. The CAA/NRC is just one example of this. However, I will also say that the unexpected results of the election, especially the losses the BJP suffered in key states like Uttar Pradesh, which is India's largest state, and among lower-caste people, show that voters are tired of the current situation of high inflation and long-term unemployment. For these voters, the ethnonationalism platform may not be "enough" to keep them interested. We hope this will prevent the ruling party from adopting excessively extreme policies.

What Does Another Modi's Term Look Like, And How Might It Impact India?

Political opponents of the regime are likely to face more frequent arrests as democracy deteriorates, leading to a reduction in protest spaces. In terms of their ethnonationalist goals, the BJP will take on the CAA/NRC even more. There will be unprecedented levels of lynching, harassment, and intimidation against Muslims and people from lower castes. The BJP will also try to finish up some unfinished business on the economic front. For example, they will try to get through a hugely unpopular change to the forest law that would make it easier for corporations to take forest land from native people.

Farmers led a 16-month protest that halted the implementation of the farm laws, but there's a chance they may try again. The election results that came as a surprise add some uncertainty to the situation, as junior ally parties will now be able to put pressure on the BJP in ways they couldn't before. But it remains to be seen if these smaller parties, or the India Block opposition parties, will be able to push for politics that are very different from the BJP's. For example, they might be able to offer alternatives to the politics of supremacy or find ways to fix the country's growing inequality.

Second, it could mean that the BJP and Modi will be different and less powerful. The parliament's increased activity should test some of the majoritarian ideas that have been central to the BJP's strategy over the past few years. It looks like voters were really worried about how the BJP would hurt liberal democracy. Liberal voters in Mumbai chose to vote against the BJP by backing the Shiv Sena, a historically right-leaning party whose faction joined the India Alliance, as an interesting example. This makes me think they want to save democracy. We will have to wait and see if this apparent opposition to some parts of the BJP's politics will last for the next five years.

Shapers Of the India's General Elections 2024

Social media and fake news, like deep-fake AI videos and hate speech, played a big part in this election. There was a lot of false information and hate speech, but for a number of reasons, it is difficult to say how much of an effect it had on the elections. First, a lot of people have talked about how the BJP has an advantage on social media, but the truth is that a lot of campaigning actually takes place at rallies in person, with people on the ground. Second, studying the impact of false information on negative outcomes remains challenging. It's not clear that people change their minds because of false information; it's more likely that individuals believe false information because of their political views and other values. In fact, it appears that the BJP lost power and failed to maintain its majority in at least two constituencies— Faizabad and Banswara— where political rhetoric and actions included spreading false information and marginalization politics. It looks like this election was more about money problems and issues that voters face every day than about ideas and identities. On a side note, Indian social media consistently features a significant amount of fake news and AI-based content. Even though people who are crazy about AI talk about possible end-of-the- world scenarios, the numbers show that this is not a major concern.

The Fall of Modi and BJP Vs the Rise of Congress Alliance Party

Experts in politics and exit polls quickly said that Narendra Modi would win this year's elections, which took place from April 19 to June

1. We now expect him to serve a third term as India's prime minister. It was up to him and his party, the Bharatiya Janata Party (BJP), to get enough votes to claim a supermajority.

As the final results came in on Tuesday, June 4, it became clear what the answer was. After counting more than half of the votes, the BJP and its National Democratic Alliance, comprising several right-wing, conservative regional parties, secured 290 seats in India's 543-seat Lok Sabha, or lower house of parliament. Modi loses the one-party majority he has held since his first election in 2014, as the alliance's predicted victory of 400 seats falls short. A big change from the BJP's huge win in 2019, when it won an unprecedented 303 seats, is that the ruling party has won only 238 seats.

The opposition India alliance, which includes the Indian National Congress and more than 20 other opposition parties, won 235 seats, which was better than expected. The final results should come out late Tuesday night or early Wednesday morning.

Any party or coalition that wins more than 272 seats in India's 543-member parliament can form a government. Over a billion Indians went to the polls over the course of six weeks, in seven stages. It was the biggest democratic election in the world.

Modi, who is 73 years old and a charismatic but divisive leader, will be in office for a rare third term in a row. Jaipur's first prime minister, Congress leader Jawaharlal Nehru, was the only other Indian prime minister to do this. Modi praised India's election process and the BJP's accomplishments in a speech at the party's headquarters in Delhi on Tuesday evening. He said, "No government has come back into power for a third time since 1962." He also said that the BJP had gotten twice as many votes in some places.

But even though Modi is likely to be able to carry out his promised Hindu-nationalist agenda and set of economic reforms, the BJP's smaller-than-expected majority means that he may face a stronger opposition than at any time in the last ten years. Unless the BJP negotiates with smaller alliances and opposition leaders, implementation will be difficult.

The Director of the South Asia Program at the Carnegie Endowment for International Peace, Milan Vaishnav, says, "This election is definitely a slap in the face for Modi and the BJP." "After ten years in power, it was like a vote on how well it did, and it's clear that a lot of Indians are feeling restless and uneasy."

India's Political Outlook and Global Turmoil

India's elections get a lot of attention worldwide because the country is becoming a bigger regional and global power. As the biggest democracy in the world, India's political decisions affect trade, geopolitical alignments, and the security of the surrounding area. India's foreign policy goals will be affected by the elections' results, especially when dealing with its complicated relationships with major powers and neighboring countries. International companies and multilateral organizations also closely monitor India's economic growth. For India's economy and the world economy, attracting foreign direct investment and growing the economy depends on a stable political atmosphere. Any indications of political unrest or unclear policies in India can impact markets around the world, lowering investor trust and the outlook for economies around the world.

Lastly, India's upcoming elections are not just a local matter; they also affect trade, economic security, and global politics. The world is paying close attention as India stands at a key point where its future will depend on its political decisions. These decisions will have an impact on the whole world.

Assessment of India's Economic Growth, Prospects, and Global Impact

The Indian economy, one of the major economies expanding at the quickest rate globally, is currently at an important turning point in its journey. The country's economic trajectory bears important implications not just for its residents but also for the larger world community as a whole. This is because the country's population is growing at an alarming rate, a tremendous amount of potential has yet to be exploited, and the global landscape is changing rapidly.

This evaluation takes a deep dive into India's current economic performance, its potential for future growth, and the ripple effects that its economic decisions have had on the international stage. It does so by utilizing facts and figures to create a comprehensive analysis.

Performance of the Economy as of Late

The economic journey India has taken over the last few decades has been marked by exceptional progress, which has been punctuated by periods of robust expansion and periodic slowdowns, respectively. In recent years, the nation has emerged as one of the leading economies in the world. This achievement results from various factors, including demographic dividends, technical innovation, and governmental reforms. However, the COVID-19 epidemic seriously affected India's economy, resulting in a reduction in the growth of the country's gross domestic product (GDP) and exacerbating structural issues already present.

A growth trajectory was followed by India's economy before the epidemic, with the country's gross domestic product rising at an average yearly rate of almost 7% in the period from 2014 to 2019. According to official figures from the Ministry of Statistics and Programme Implementation, the pandemic's beginning in 2020 resulted in a significant contraction, with the gross domestic product (GDP) decreasing by 7.3% in the fiscal year 2020-21 after the epidemic began. The disruptions in supply chains, the decrease in consumer spending, and the drop-in investment activity were the primary factors that led to this downturn.

Despite the difficulties brought about by the epidemic, India has shown that it has the tenacity and adaptability necessary to recover economically. There are indications that high-frequency indicators indicate a revival in economic activity, with numerous industries, including manufacturing, agriculture, and services, exhibiting signs of recovery. The International Monetary Fund (IMF) forecasts that India's gross domestic product (GDP) will expand by 9.5% in the fiscal year 2021-22, making it the major economy with the fastest growth rate in the world, despite starting from a low foundation.

The World in Turmoil

Growth Opportunities shortly

India's economic prospects remain optimistic, boosted by favorable demographic trends, a dynamic entrepreneurial ecosystem, and ongoing structural reforms. Looking ahead, India's economic prospects also remain positive. Several ambitious projects, including "Make in India," "Digital India," and "Atmanirbhar Bharat" (self-reliant India), have been launched by the government to foster domestic manufacturing, improve digital infrastructure, and encourage entrepreneurial endeavors. These initiatives are intended to build the groundwork for sustainable and long-term growth.

A huge opportunity for economic transformation and inclusive development is presented by India's demographic dividend, which consists of a youthful and aspirational population. With investments in education, skill development, and innovation, India can unlock new pathways of growth and productivity enhancement. This may be accomplished by leveraging the potential of its young people.

Additionally, India's growing integration into global value chains and its position as a popular destination for foreign direct investment (FDI) offer new opportunities for economic advancement. Both of these developments could be beneficial to India's economy. Multiple international firms looking to diversify their operations and enter new markets will find the country an interesting option due to its strategic location, big consumer base, and competitive labor prices.

Assessment of Regional and Global Implications of India's Policies and Developments Not only do India's policies and developments have a big influence within its borders, but they also have a considerable influence on the regional and global arenas simultaneously. Given that India is the largest democracy in the world and one of the major economies that is developing at the quickest rate, its decisions have repercussions in the geopolitical, economic, and social spheres. This evaluation aims to provide a complete study by utilizing facts and statistics to investigate the effects of India's policies and developments on a regional and global scale.

Impact on the Economy:

India's economic policies and performance have significant repercussions for the neighboring area and the entire world. India has a nominal gross domestic product (GDP) greater than $2.8 trillion, making it the sixth-largest economy in the world as of 2021. In spite of the fact that the COVID-19 epidemic has affected its economic growth trajectory, it continues to be robust compared to the majority of other large economies.

Regional Implications:

The expansion of India's economy is a driving force behind the development of the surrounding region, particularly in South Asia. India, which has the largest economy in the region, plays a crucial role in the development of infrastructure, as well as in the promotion of commerce and investment among the countries that form its immediate vicinity. As a result of initiatives such as the South Asian Association for Regional Cooperation (SAARC) and the Bay of Bengal Initiative for Multi-Sectoral Technical and Economic Cooperation (BIMSTEC), India has demonstrated its dedication to promoting regional cooperation and integration.

Global Implications:

The rise of India's economy has established it as a significant player in the economics of the entire world. Through its membership in organizations such as the Group of Twenty (G20) and the BRICS (Brazil, Russia, India, China, and South Africa), India can actively participate in formulating worldwide economic policies and resolving global issues. In addition, India's sizable consumer market offers lucrative chances for international firms looking to expand their operations, making the country an appealing location for foreign investment.

Aspects of Geopolitical Action:

The geopolitical posture of India and the strategic decisions it makes have potentially far- reaching ramifications for the stability of the region and the dynamics of global power. India's activities significantly impact the security calculations of its surrounding countries and the big powers because of its geostrategic location and gradually expanding military capability.

Regional Implications:

Complex geopolitical dynamics are a defining characteristic of India's ties with its surrounding countries, particularly Pakistan and China. Tensions along the border between India and Pakistan, as well as the Kashmir dispute that has not been addressed, have long-term ramifications for the stability of the area. In a similar vein, the border issues that India has with China, particularly along the Line of Actual Control (LAC), have the potential to grow into more extensive confrontations that might have important repercussions for the security of the area.

Global Implications:

India's developing strategic engagement with the United States and other major countries, which is motivated by shared interests in counterterrorism, maritime security, and economic cooperation, has consequences for the dynamics of power on a global scale. India, a significant member of the Quad, consisting of the United States of America, Japan, Australia, and India, participates in efforts to maintain a free, open, and inclusive Indo-Pacific area. These efforts are a response to China's assertive behavior in the region.

Environment Impact:

Environmental policies and development decisions made by India have substantial repercussions for ecosystems in the surrounding region and for efforts to mitigate the effects of climate change on a global scale. India's steps to transition towards renewable energy and address environmental concerns are keenly monitored by the international community. India is one of the top producers of greenhouse gases in the world.

Regional Implications:

India's environmental policies affect the air and water quality in the region, as well as the conservation of biodiversity and the management of natural resources. Industrial pollution, vehicle emissions, and agricultural practices all contribute to pollution that impacts not only cities in India but also the nations adjacent to India, particularly in the Indo-Gangetic Plain region. India's dedication to addressing environmental concerns in the region through multilateral collaboration is highlighted by collaborative projects such as the International Solar Alliance (ISA), which India and France initiated.

Global Implications:

Due to the size of its population, the trajectory of its economic growth, and the patterns of its energy consumption, India plays an extremely important role in worldwide efforts to mitigate the effects of climate change. The nation's commitment to cut carbon emissions and increase the proportion of renewable energy in the entire energy mix, as stipulated by the Paris Agreement, contributes to the overall efforts being made worldwide to address climate change. Furthermore, India's leadership in programs such as the Coalition for Disaster Resilient Infrastructure (CDRI) demonstrates the country's dedication to strengthening global resilience to hazards associated with climate change.

Social and Cultural Influence:

As a result of its diversified society and extensive cultural legacy, India can wield soft power influence both regionally and worldwide. India promotes its values, traditions, and cultural exports internationally through its efforts in cultural diplomacy and connection with the diaspora.

Regional Implications:

Indian movies, music, literature, and food all have a significant impact on popular culture across boundaries, demonstrating India's cultural dominance. This influence extends throughout the South Asian region. Bollywood films, in particular, enjoy broad popularity in nations that are geographically close to them, which helps to promote cultural connectivity and participation among individuals from different backgrounds.

India's cultural exports are reaching audiences worldwide, demonstrating that India's soft power extends beyond South Asia. Yoga, Ayurveda, Indian cuisine, and traditional arts and crafts are all aspects of India's cultural legacy and diversity that are becoming increasingly popular worldwide. Additionally, India's diaspora, consisting of more than 30 million individuals, acts as a bridge between India and the global community, contributing to the interchange of cultural ideas, trade, and investment.

A conclusion may be drawn that India's policies and activities have a variety of repercussions for the country and the world at large. India's actions have a significant impact on the dynamics of the region and the consequences of global events, whether economic, geopolitical, environmental, or social. India has the potential to play a constructive role in strengthening regional cooperation, tackling global difficulties, and crafting a more prosperous and secure future for all people if it capitalizes on its assets and takes proactive measures to solve challenges.

Chapter 5: Pakistan's Elections and Economic Challenges

Insights into recent elections in Pakistan and their outcomes

The 2024 elections in Pakistan were a significant turning point characterized by a convergence of political turmoil and a worsening economic crisis. This essay examines the fundamental characteristics of the elections, the financial difficulties afflicting the country, and the interconnectedness of these elements that endanger Pakistan's stability.

The Election Riddled with Conflict: A Country Split Apart

The February 2024 elections were tainted by scandal. The ousting of ex-Prime Minister Imran Khan in 2022 has significant implications, as allegations of political meddling and manipulation of the democratic system accompanied it. Although no political party obtained an outright majority, a delicate coalition government was formed, with the Pakistan Muslim League-Nawaz (PML-N) and Pakistan Peoples Party (PPP) at the helm. The result of the election caused the electorate to become even more divided, as Imran Khan's Pakistan Tehreek-e-Insaf (PTI) party strongly challenged the results and organized street protests. The possibility of political instability was significant, threatening any efforts to achieve economic recovery.

The Economic Maelstrom: A Perfect Storm

Pakistan's economic position before the elections was unstable. Below is an analysis of the primary obstacles:

Rapidly increasing inflation:

The inflation rate surged to more than 30%, causing a decline in purchasing power and resulting in the impoverishment of millions of people. The increase was driven by a confluence of circumstances, such as the rupee devaluation, escalating global commodity costs, and disruptions in the supply chain.

Overwhelming Financial Obligation:

Pakistan's external debt commitments have reached a concerning magnitude, with billions of dollars that must be repaid by the end of 2024. This constraint hindered the government's capacity to allocate funds towards critical sectors such as healthcare and education.

Elevated unemployment:

There needs to be more growth in job opportunities and increasing unemployment rates, especially among young people. The social upheaval exacerbated the already precarious economy.

Energy Crisis:

Pakistan has a persistent energy deficit, resulting in frequent power cuts and impeding industrial efficiency. This exacerbated the decline in economic growth.

The Intertwined Crisis:

The current situation can be described as a complex crisis characterized by political uncertainty and economic stagnation.

The political instability surrounding the elections worsened the economic situation. A robust and consistent government could have helped the implementation of enduring economic reforms and the ability to engage in negotiations with international lenders such as the IMF. The demonstrations and the possibility of additional political turmoil deterred foreign investment, a vital source of finance for Pakistan's progress.

Potential Courses of Action: Maneuvering in Economic Turbulent Conditions in Pakistan

The newly formed coalition government is confronted with a formidable challenge. Here are several possible courses of action:

International Monetary Fund (IMF) Financial Assistance and Measures to Reduce Government Spending:

Obtaining financial assistance from the International Monetary Fund (IMF) may be important to restore economic stability. However, these conditions frequently entail strict measures such as reductions in subsidies and increases in taxes, which can impose further financial strain on the population. The administration must carefully balance maintaining economic discipline and preventing civil upheaval.

Emphasize the importance of exports and investment:

Enhancing exports and enticing foreign investment is vital for enhancing Pakistan's foreign exchange reserves and generating employment opportunities. This necessitates simplifying rules, enhancing infrastructure, and establishing a more conducive climate for business.

Addressing Corruption and Bureaucracy:

Rampant corruption and a burdensome bureaucracy impede economic progress. The government must adopt efficient anti-corruption strategies and optimize administrative procedures to enhance resource allocation and attract investment.

Human capital investment:

Allocating resources towards education and healthcare will enhance the workforce's capabilities and improve Pakistan's economic prospects in the long run. This involves nurturing a highly proficient workforce capable of competing in the international market.

Political reconciliation:

Resolving the existing political polarization is essential for ensuring enduring stability. Facilitating open communication and establishing agreement on crucial economic reforms guarantees national cohesion.

The 2024 elections in Pakistan and the resulting economic upheaval significantly challenge the nation's resiliency. The new government's success depends on its capacity to confront the financial crisis directly while manoeuvring through a tumultuous political environment. For Pakistan to navigate towards a more prosperous and secure future, it is crucial to establish connections between different political ideologies, adopt effective economic strategies, and address long-standing difficulties.

Regional Powers and Pakistan's Election 2024

The 2024 elections in Pakistan had implications beyond the country's borders. As regional powers, China, the United States, and India exert significant influence and actively pursue their interests. Below is an analysis of their interests and possible impact on the political environment, as presented in "The Players and their Games".

- China:

China, a strong supporter of Pakistan, primarily focuses on safeguarding its investments in the China-Pakistan Economic Corridor (CPEC). The success of this vast infrastructure project relies heavily on Pakistan's stability. China may have discreetly applied influence to ensure the continuity of a government that supports the advancement of the China- Pakistan Economic Corridor (CPEC).

Stakeholders:

The Pakistani government: depends on Chinese financial assistance for the construction of infrastructure but is subjected to public scrutiny due to concerns about transparency and the weight of debt.

Local Communities: Due to the impact of CPEC projects, individuals may pursue compensation and demand environmental protection.

- The United States:

The United States has a multifaceted relationship with Pakistan, aiming to collaborate on counterterrorism initiatives but remaining cautious of its affiliations with China and the Taliban regime in Afghanistan. The United States may have preferred an administration perceived as more closely aligned with its regional security interests.

Parties with a vested interest:

Pakistan Armed Forces: Has a lengthy history of cooperation with the United States and may prefer an ongoing partnership.

Hostility towards the United States: A portion of the populace may regard the involvement of the United States as interference in domestic politics.

- India:

The country has a strained relationship with Pakistan. An Afghanistan administration that is stable and aligned with Pakistan's interests may jeopardize India's security. India may have desired a Pakistani administration that is less inclined to help the Taliban.

Stakeholders:

Kashmiri secessionist groups: May request assistance from a Pakistani government that supports their goals.

Pakistan Business Community: Seeks to enhance trade links with India to reap economic advantages.

The Above Countries Influence on the Pakistan's Elections

The influence of regional powers is a challenging task. Nevertheless, their acts may have subtly influenced the elections in the following manners:

Monetary assistance:

China may have indirectly affected the outcome by providing financial or political support to favoured political parties.

Political Communication:

Regional states may have utilized diplomatic channels to communicate their desires to Pakistani political authorities.

Manipulation of the media:

Regional powers may employ media outlets to manipulate public opinion in their favour. Indeterminate Results:

The precise influence of regional powers continues to be discussed. The Pakistani electorate ultimately chose the governing body. However, national security concerns and the desire for economic alliances impacted political calculations.

Progressing ahead:

The nascent administration in Pakistan will need to deftly manoeuvre the intricate dynamics with neighbouring influential nations while giving precedence to its domestic concerns.

Striking a balance between different interests:

Pakistan must cultivate positive relationships with all influential entities while ensuring their engagement contributes to the nation's advancement.

Openness in Transactions:

Confidential deals with regional powers might contribute to public scepticism. Enhanced transparency can strengthen public trust in the government's decision-making process. Preventing Proxy Conflicts:

Pakistan must avoid becoming a theatre for regional conflicts.

Regional powers undoubtedly exert influence over Pakistan's political scene. The Pakistani government must identify and strategically manage its interests to establish an independent direction and guarantee a stable and prosperous future.

The Maelstrom of Uncertainty: Turmoil Following Pakistan's 2024 Elections

The aftermath of Pakistan's 2024 elections has been marked by substantial upheaval, characterized by various crucial elements:

Disputed results and allegations of manipulation:

The tight competition and absence of a distinct majority for any political party prompted allegations of electoral rigging. The PTI party led by Imran Khan strongly challenged the results, alleging extensive irregularities. This fostered an atmosphere of suspicion and undermined the credibility of the result from the perspective of a considerable segment of the populace.

Social demonstrations and governmental unrest:

Many of Khan's followers mobilized and participated in widespread demonstrations, resulting in nationwide protests. Occasionally, these rallies escalated into violence, causing worries about societal instability and possible confrontations with security personnel. The delicate coalition administration faced difficulties in upholding stability amid the ongoing demonstrations.

Increasing Polarization:

The disputed elections intensified the pre-existing political rifts in Pakistan. Advocates of many political parties participated in acrimonious online and offline discussions, exacerbating the division and impeding any possibility of political reconciliation. This entrenched political position made establishing consensus on crucial national matters challenging.

Economic Impact:

The political instability deterred foreign investment and impeded economic growth. Investors maintained caution in allocating resources until a stable government materialized and tackled urgent economic issues effectively. This exacerbated Pakistan's already precarious financial status.

Diminished global reputation:

The electoral unrest conveyed an impression of volatility on the international platform. This may impact Pakistan's capacity to attract foreign aid and investment, impeding its endeavours for economic progress.

Possible escalation:

The protracted political impasse may result in additional escalation. Failure to address tensions can escalate violence, impeding advancements in crucial economic and social changes.

Desire for a Solution:

Amidst the present upheaval, there exist potential avenues for progress: Discussion and resolution of conflicts:

Enabling communication between the administration and opposition leaders could facilitate the resolution of political differences and allow for the possibility of settling. Enhancing the effectiveness and resilience of democratic institutions:

Implementing measures to improve public trust in the electoral process, such as establishing impartial election oversight and adopting transparent vote tabulation, is essential for ensuring future stability.

Direct attention towards the most important goals and objectives of the nation:

All parties must prioritize the nation's interests and collaborate to tackle urgent economic and social concerns.

In conclusion, the 2024 elections in Pakistan were pivotal and revealed significant divisions throughout the country's society and political landscape. For Pakistan to overcome the current era of instability and achieve a more prosperous future, it is crucial to address the underlying reasons for the turbulence and promote open communication.

Comparison of Pakistan with Its Adjacent Nations

In South Asia, Pakistan has a multifaceted economy in which the agriculture, industry, and services sectors hold prominent positions. Throughout its history, the nation has had various economic difficulties, such as political instability, security issues, insufficient energy supply, and fiscal deficits. Nevertheless, it has also exhibited durability and capacity for expansion, bolstered by its substantial population, advantageous geographical position, and abundant natural resources.

Economic Overview:

Agriculture:

Pakistan's economy mostly relies on agriculture, with key industries such as cotton, wheat, rice, and sugarcane making substantial contributions to its gross domestic product (GDP). A significant proportion of the labor force, especially in rural regions, is employed in the agricultural sector.

Industry:

Pakistan's industrial sector is expanding and includes manufacturing, textiles, chemicals, and construction. The industrial sector is vital for economic development and the creation of jobs.

Available services:

Pakistan's economy relies heavily on the services sector, which includes crucial industries like finance, telecommunications, retail, and tourism. Karachi, the country's largest metropolis, is a significant center for finance and commerce.

Remittances:

Pakistan receives significant remittances from its diaspora, namely from nations such as the United Arab Emirates, Saudi Arabia, and the

United States. Remittances substantially contribute to the country's foreign exchange reserves and the incomes of households.

Obstacles:

Pakistan encounters many economic barriers, such as inflation, unemployment, budget deficits, corruption, and infrastructure shortages. Furthermore, the nation's security condition and geopolitical conflicts present potential hazards to economic stability and prosperity.

Factors Affecting Pakistan's Gross Domestic Product (Gdp):

Public policies implemented by the government:

The GDP of Pakistan can be significantly influenced by government policies about taxation, investment, trade, and subsidies. Implementing pro-business reforms, investing in infrastructure development, and implementing steps to improve the ease of doing business have the potential to stimulate economic growth.

Global economic conditions:

Pakistan's economy is impacted by worldwide economic trends, such as volatility in commodity prices, alterations in international trade dynamics, and changes in global demand. Economic slowdowns or recessions in significant economies can impact Pakistan's exports and remittances.

Monetary policy:

The State Bank of Pakistan, which serves as the nation's central bank, is vital in overseeing monetary policy to regulate inflation, maintain currency stability, and foster economic expansion. Interest rate and liquidity management changes in the banking system impact investment and consumption patterns, affecting GDP growth.

Development of physical structures and systems:

Investments in infrastructure, such as transportation, energy, and telecommunications, are crucial for promoting economic growth and improving productivity. Enhancements in infrastructure have the potential to decrease transportation expenses, streamline trade processes, and entice investments in essential industries.

Societal influences:

Population growth, literacy rates, healthcare availability, and income distribution are socio-economic factors that affect Pakistan's GDP. Allocating resources toward education, healthcare, and social welfare programs has the potential to enhance human capital and productivity, hence fostering sustainable economic growth in the long run.

Factors originating from outside sources:

Geopolitical tensions, regional wars, and international relations can influence Pakistan's economy. The relations with neighboring nations, namely India and Afghanistan, and the broader geopolitical landscape influence investor confidence, trade flows, and foreign direct investment.

Comparing the Economics of Pakistan and Its Neighbors

Analyzing Pakistan's economy and neighboring countries provides valuable insights into the area's economic dynamics, difficulties, and prospects. This analysis will compare Pakistan and its neighboring countries: India, Afghanistan, Iran, and China.

1.India:

Similarities:

A. Pakistan and India possess substantial populations, rendering them noteworthy consumer markets and labor pools.

B. Both nations possess diverse economies that contribute substantially from the agricultural, industrial, and services sectors.

C. Both countries encounter obstacles with infrastructure development, income disparity, and social imbalances.

Contrasts:

D. India has a far larger economy than Pakistan, characterized by a more varied industrial foundation, a more robust services sector, and a greater GDP per capita.

E. India has consistently achieved a higher economic growth rate than Pakistan in recent years despite both countries encountering similar obstacles, such as unemployment and poverty.

F. India possesses a highly advanced financial and technological sector characterized by a burgeoning focus on innovation and entrepreneurship.

2. Afghanistan:

Similarities:

G. Pakistan and Afghanistan are primarily rural economies, where agriculture plays a crucial role in supporting the livelihoods of the inhabitants.

H. Both nations encounter security, political volatility, and difficulties with economic advancement.

Contrasts:

I. Afghanistan's economy is substantially smaller than Pakistan's and mainly depends on international aid and remittances.

J. Pakistan possesses a more varied industrial and services sector in comparison to Afghanistan, which is now in the process of recovering after numerous years of conflict.

K. Pakistan plays a significant role as a primary pathway for trade between Afghanistan and other countries. This arrangement brings economic advantages and difficulties for both nations.

3. Iran:

Similarities:

L. Pakistan and Iran both have substantial populations and possess cultural and historical connections.

M. Both nations encounter economic difficulties from sanctions, energy deficits, and unemployment.

Contrasts:

N. Iran's economy surpasses that of Pakistan, boasting a more advanced industrial foundation and substantial oil and gas deposits.

O. Pakistan has a more diverse economy than Iran, which mainly depends on revenue generated from oil exports.

P. Pakistan encounters security obstacles concerning its border with Iran, encompassing illicit trade and conflicts over the border.

4. China: Similarities:

Q. Pakistan and China are neighboring countries with strong diplomatic and commercial relations.

R. Both nations have initiated infrastructure development initiatives, such as the China-Pakistan Economic Corridor (CPEC), to improve connectivity and foster economic collaboration.

Contrasts:

S. China possesses one of the most substantial and rapidly expanding economies globally, but Pakistan's economy is comparatively smaller and encounters inherent structural obstacles.

T. China serves as a prominent worldwide center for manufacturing and exporting, but Pakistan's industrial sector is comparatively underdeveloped and has challenges in terms of competitiveness.

U. China has made substantial investments in Pakistan's infrastructure and energy sector, which can enhance Pakistan's long-term economic growth.

To summarize, although Pakistan has certain parallels with its neighboring countries regarding demographic features and economic issues, there are notable distinctions in economic size, structure, and development priorities. Enhancing regional collaboration, tackling shared obstacles, and capitalizing on each other's capabilities could open prospects for financial expansion and well-being in the region.

Possible Factors and Countries Contributing To the Decline of Pakistan's Economy

Pakistan's economy is currently facing challenges due to domestic and international issues. Although it would be incorrect to ascribe the decline to other countries entirely, external circumstances and diplomatic relations with specific nations have influenced the situation. Below are a few countries and their actions or relationships that have impacted Pakistan's economic crisis:

1. United States:

Effect:

The United States has played a substantial role in Pakistan's economy by providing financial assistance and investing.

Nevertheless, the tense relations between the two nations, primarily stemming from divergent counter-terrorism approaches, have resulted in oscillations in the level of U.S. aid and investor trust in Pakistan.

The suspension of military aid by the United States and the imposition of sanctions on certain Pakistani businesses have significantly impacted Pakistan's defense sector and overall investor sentiment.

2. China:

Impact:

China's impact on Pakistan has been significant, primarily due to programs such as the China-Pakistan Economic Corridor (CPEC). China has become a crucial economic ally for Pakistan.

Although the China-Pakistan Economic Corridor (CPEC) has substantial prospects for infrastructure development in Pakistan, it also poses specific difficulties, such as the buildup of debt, apprehensions over transparency, and the possibility of becoming overly reliant on China.

Pakistan's economy could be affected by the economic deceleration in China or shifts in its investment preferences, considering Pakistan's dependence on Chinese funding and initiatives.

3. India:

Impact:

Pakistan and India have a protracted rivalry, frequently resulting in economic frictions and wars.

The presence of trade disputes, border conflicts, and political difficulties has impeded the process of regional economic integration and stability between the two countries.

India's withdrawal of Article 370, altering the unique status of Jammu and Kashmir, exacerbated tensions between the two nations, impacting bilateral trade and economic collaboration.

4. Eastern Mediterranean Countries:

Impact:

Pakistan benefits greatly from substantial remittances from its diaspora employed in Middle Eastern nations, notably Saudi Arabia, the United Arab Emirates, and Qatar.

Volatility in oil prices and economic circumstances in the Middle East can impact the amount of money sent as remittances to Pakistan, which in turn affects the earnings of households and the country's external balances.

Pakistan's economic policies and regional dynamics can be influenced by its connections with specific Middle Eastern nations, such as Saudi Arabia and Iran.

5. Impact of International Financial Institutions:

Effect:

Pakistan's economic policies and ability to obtain financial aid have been shaped by its interactions with international financial institutions such as the International Monetary Fund (IMF).

Pakistan's interaction with the International Monetary Fund (IMF), which includes borrowing programs and conditions for structural adjustments, has influenced its fiscal and monetary policies and added to its debt burden.

The negative evaluations from credit rating agencies, which are frequently affected by economic and political considerations, can significantly impact investor confidence in Pakistan's economy and its ability to access international capital markets.

Ultimately, Pakistan's economic issues are influenced by local policy and external forces, with connections with other countries playing a crucial role. Deteriorated diplomatic relations, commercial conflicts, and geopolitical strains have the potential to impede economic collaboration and stability. In contrast, alliances with essential allies and financial counterparts can present prospects for expansion and progress. To address its economic issues and achieve its growth potential, Pakistan must prioritize maintaining diplomatic relations and implementing solid economic policies.

Chapter 6: South American Shifts: Brazil, Mexico, and Changing Dynamics

In the intricate geopolitical terrain of South America, alliances and dynamics are ever-changing for many reasons, spanning from economic interests to political ideologies. In recent years, notable transformations have altered the alliances and power dynamics in the region. South America is experiencing a significant revolution reshaping its interactions with regional and global entities. This transformation includes emerging new leaders, economic crises, and shifting global dynamics. This dynamic nature is propelled by various elements, which encompass:

V. The rise of new global powers: The increasing economic influence of China and the assertive foreign policy of Russia provide South American nations with various options for partnerships in addition to the United States.

W. Ideological divisions: The oscillation of political power between left-wing and right- wing governments directly influences the collaborative endeavors of different regions.

X. Political instability within a country: The current state of economic concerns and societal instability is leading to a reevaluation of the priorities in foreign policy.

Examination of recent developments in South American countries

A significant transformation in the political environment of important nations like Brazil and Argentina has occurred recently. The ascension of Jair Bolsonaro in Brazil and Alberto Fernández in Argentina has brought about fresh dynamics within the region. Bolsonaro's right-wing and populist agenda has resulted in strengthened relations with the United States and damaged relations with longstanding allies such as Venezuela and Cuba. Furthermore, Fernández's triumph signifies a resurgence of Peronist governance in Argentina, indicating a departure from the neoliberal strategies implemented by the last administration and perhaps fostering stronger alliances with leftist governments in the area.

Venezuela's enduring political and economic crisis has had notable repercussions on regional alliances. Under Nicolás Maduro's leadership, the Venezuelan economy has experienced a severe decline, resulting in a large number of Venezuelans fleeing to neighboring nations and causing tensions with longstanding allies such as Bolivia and Nicaragua. Multiple countries, including the United States, have supported Juan Guaidó, the Venezuelan opposition leader. This support has resulted in further isolation of Maduro's regime and reconfiguring regional alliances.

Economic concerns have substantially influenced the formation of coalitions in South America. The region's dependence on the export of commodities, namely oil and minerals, has rendered it susceptible to swings in global commodity prices. Countries such as Brazil and Argentina have endeavored to broaden their economies and diminish their reliance on commodities exports by allocating resources to infrastructure development and manufacturing. As a result, South American countries have developed stronger economic connections with countries such as China, which has become a significant trading ally for many of them.

The increasing influence of China in the region has sparked concerns among certain countries, notably the United States, which perceives China as a strategic rival. The United States has endeavored to mitigate China's sway in South America by implementing the "America First" strategy and the creation of the Development Finance Corporation (DFC), which attempts to stimulate private sector investment in the region. Nevertheless, certain nations in South America, namely those grappling with economic difficulties, have shown a willingness to accept China's investments and have embraced stronger connections with Beijing.

Regional security concerns have influenced alliances in South America alongside economic factors. The emergence of multinational crime syndicates engaged in drug trafficking, human trafficking, and other unlawful pursuits has presented a substantial menace to regional stability. Nations such as Colombia have requested aid from the United States and other partners to battle these criminal organizations, utilizing initiatives such as Plan Colombia. Simultaneously, the ongoing crisis in Venezuela has sparked apprehensions regarding the possibility of regional unrest, leading neighboring nations to enhance their borders and bolster security cooperation.

The COVID-19 epidemic has worsened preexisting difficulties in South America and emphasized regional collaboration's significance in tackling shared dangers. The pandemic has placed significant pressure on healthcare systems and the economy throughout the region, resulting in demands for enhanced cooperation over matters such as vaccination distribution and economic revitalization. The Union of South American Nations (UNASUR) and the Community of Latin American and Caribbean States (CELAC) have aimed to synchronize regional efforts in addressing the pandemic and foster unity among member nations.

Ultimately, South America's changing alliances and dynamics result from an intricate interaction of political, economic, and security issues. The emergence of new leaders, financial difficulties, and shifting global dynamics have transformed conventional alliances and generated fresh prospects for regional collaboration and contention. To overcome the challenges faced by South America, it is imperative for the countries in the region to collaborate and tackle shared risks to establish a more secure and prosperous future.

The Waning Influence of the United States in South America

The United States has had a significant impact on the geopolitics of South America for most of the 20th century. Nevertheless, in recent years, an observable pattern suggests a decrease in American influence in the region. Multiple causes contribute to this transition, such as alterations in worldwide dynamics, changes in domestic politics within South American nations, and the development of regional alliances.

The rise of alternative global powers, particularly China, is crucial in the fall of American dominance in South America. China's exponential economic growth in recent decades has facilitated its international expansion, particularly in South America. China's significant investments, infrastructure projects, and trade agreements have positioned it as a formidable contender, challenging the longstanding American hegemony.

Chinese investments in South America typically have fewer conditions attached compared to those from the United States, making them more attractive to some countries in the region. In addition, China's Belt and Road Initiative (BRI) has created prospects for South American nations to engage in extensive infrastructure ventures that can enhance economic growth. As a result, certain countries have shifted their focus towards China and moved away from the United States.

The declining influence of the United States in South America is also heavily influenced by economic issues. The 2008 global financial crisis and the following economic downturns have exposed the weaknesses of South American economies that mainly depend on the exportation of commodities. Consequently, there has been a growing demand for diversification and regional integration to decrease reliance on external forces such as the United States.

In addition, the changing foreign policy interests of the United States have also played a role in reducing its influence in South America. Recently, the United States has shifted its focus to other regions, such as the Middle East and East Asia, diverting resources and attention away from South America. This has generated prospects for other dominant nations, such as China and Russia, to augment their regional sway.

Domestic political changes in South American countries have furthered the declining influence of the United States. The ascendance of left-wing administrations in nations such as Venezuela, Bolivia, and Ecuador during the early 21st century resulted in tense ties with the United States, as these governments implemented policies that frequently contradicted American interests. Although more centrist or right-wing administrations have replaced several South American governments, the enduring presence of anti- American ism remains in specific sectors of South American society.

Furthermore, the United States' erratic stance on democracy and human rights in the region has eroded its credibility and influence. Occurrences of U.S. interference in the domestic affairs of South American states, including backing coups or authoritarian governments, have generated hatred and suspicion towards the United States among certain South American countries.

South American countries have been actively striving to establish their independence and autonomy on the global stage as the influence of the United States diminishes. The Union of South American Nations (UNASUR) and the Community of Latin American and Caribbean States (CELAC) strive to foster regional integration and collaboration while diminishing dependence on external forces.

Ultimately, the diminishing impact of the United States in South America is a complex occurrence influenced by a blend of worldwide, regional, and domestic elements. Although the United States continues to have significance in the region, its supremacy is being contested by rising powers such as China and by changing political dynamics and priorities within South American nations. As South America maintains its autonomy and pursues its objectives, the distribution of power in the region is expected to keep changing in the future.

The Rise of New Partnerships in South America

South American countries have been taking more initiative in forming new alliances to meet their many requirements, including economic growth, infrastructural development, security, and regional unity. These collaborations demonstrate the region's changing dynamics and the South American countries' intention to broaden their alliances while pursuing their own national goals. Here are some instances of South American countries that have established new partnerships to meet their requirements:

a. Brazil-China Economic Cooperation:

Brazil, the most prominent economy in South America, has been aggressively pursuing collaborations to bolster its economic expansion and progress. A notable collaboration has been established with China, emerging as Brazil's primary trading ally. China has made significant investments in Brazilian infrastructure projects, including ports, trains, and energy facilities, establishing solid commercial relations between the two countries. Conversely, Brazil exports soybeans, iron ore, and oil to China. This collaboration has enhanced Brazil's economic expansion and contributed to China's strategic objectives in ensuring access to crucial natural resources.

b. The Chile-Pacific Alliance Trade Bloc:

Chile has played a significant role in establishing the Pacific Alliance, a regional trade group created in 2011 that comprises Mexico, Colombia, and Peru. The primary objective of the Pacific Alliance is to facilitate and enhance commercial transactions and financial commitments between its member nations while also fostering closer economic relationships with countries in the Asia-Pacific region. With its robust economy focused on exporting goods, Chile has experienced advantages from expanded market opportunities in Asia due to its participation in the Pacific Alliance. The bloc has also fostered collaboration on innovation, entrepreneurship, and sustainable development, aiding Chile in broadening its economy and diminishing its reliance on conventional markets.

c. Colombia-United States Security Cooperation:

Colombia has established a strong alliance with the United States in security and anti- narcotics operations. The United States has offered military and financial aid to Colombia through programs such as Plan Colombia to combat drug trafficking, insurgency, and organized crime. Colombia has substantially improved in reducing violence and stabilizing regions devastated by conflict, thanks to our relationship. Additionally, it has enhanced the mutual relations between the two nations, establishing Colombia as a significant ally of the United States in the region.

d. Argentina-Russia Nuclear Energy Cooperation:

Argentina has sought collaboration with nations like Russia to enhance its nuclear energy capability. INVAP, Argentina's government-owned atomic corporation, has partnered with Rosatom, Russia's state-owned nuclear energy firm, to create nuclear power facilities and research reactors jointly. An outstanding endeavor is the ongoing construction of the Atucha III nuclear power station, undertaken with Russian support. This alliance seeks to bolster Argentina's energy security while augmenting its technological prowess in the nuclear industry.

e. Ecuador-Iran Infrastructure Development:

Ecuador has actively pursued collaborations with nations such as Iran to bolster its infrastructure development initiatives. Iran has offered financial and technical support to Ecuador for many initiatives, including the development of roads, hydroelectric dams, and oil refineries. The collaboration has enabled Ecuador to secure financing and specialized knowledge for vital infrastructure initiatives, promoting economic expansion and generating job prospects. Nevertheless, it has faced criticism from certain factions, notably the United States, which has expressed apprehensions regarding Iran's engagement in the region.

f. Bolivia-Cuba Healthcare Cooperation:

Bolivia has forged strong connections with Cuba, namely in healthcare. Bolivia has received Cuban medical expertise and support through programs like "Operation Miracle," which offers free eye operations to low-income individuals. Cuban doctors and healthcare professionals have been dispatched to Bolivia to deliver medical services in rural areas lacking adequate healthcare access. This collaboration has not only enhanced the availability of healthcare for the people of Bolivia but has also bolstered the diplomatic relations between the two nations.

g. Peru-India Defense Cooperation:

In recent years, Peru has strengthened its defense collaboration with India, focusing on military training and exchanging technological expertise. The two nations have entered into agreements to cooperate on defense research and development and to carry out joint military exercises. This relationship aims to strengthen Peru's defense capabilities and update its armed forces by procuring Indian military equipment and technologies. Additionally, it demonstrates Peru's endeavors to broaden its defense collaborations beyond conventional allies such as the United States.

These examples demonstrate the wide variety of collaborations South American countries have established to tackle their distinct requirements and goals. These relationships encompass various areas, including economic cooperation, infrastructure development, security, and healthcare. They demonstrate the intricate and changing dynamics of the region as governments aim to utilize external resources and expertise to promote their own national goals. As South America faces the difficulties of the 21st century, these alliances are expected to greatly influence the region's future direction.

Implications of shifting alliances and economic dynamics in South America

The ramifications of changing alliances and economic dynamics in South America are complex and have extensive implications for the region's political stability, economic growth, and geopolitical landscape. These changes can alter the ties between countries in South America and their engagement with global powers. Here are some significant consequences of these changes:

1.Geopolitical Realignment:

The changing alliances in South America are causing a reorganization of geopolitical interests in the region. Conventional partnerships, such as those with the United States, are confronted by novel collaborations with rising powers such as China and Russia. This realignment could alter the distribution of power among different regions and impact the equilibrium of power in South America.

2. Economic Prospects and Obstacles:

South American countries can seize the chance to broaden their economy and gain entry into untapped markets by establishing fresh economic alliances. For instance, establishing stronger connections with China can grant us opportunities to acquire investment, technology, and infrastructure development. Nevertheless, depending solely on one trading partner can also provide vulnerabilities, as evidenced by the economic downturns encountered by nations that significantly rely on commodity exports during periods of global market volatility.

3. Infrastructure Development:

Economic collaborations frequently entail initiatives to enhance transportation, electricity, and telecommunications networks through infrastructure development projects. Although these projects have the potential to foster economic growth and improve regional connectivity, they may also give rise to apprehensions over environmental sustainability, social inclusion, and reliance on debt if not effectively managed.

4. Security ramifications:

Changes in alliances can impact the dynamics of regional security. Enhanced diplomatic relations with major global powers such as China and Russia could result in heightened military collaboration and the possible escalation of arms trade, perhaps worsening current tensions or instigating arms races in the region. In addition, altering alliances can affect regional endeavors to combat cross-border security challenges such as drug trafficking, organized crime, and terrorism.

5. Political Stability and Governance:

Shifts in alliances and economic dynamics can potentially impact South American nations' political stability and administration. For instance, governments that significantly depend on external assistance may experience pressure to conform their domestic policies to their foreign counterparts' preferences, which might weaken democratic institutions and accountability. Furthermore, the rivalry for resources and control between external powers can intensify political division and conflicts within nations.

6.Regional integration:

Alliance changes can either support or impede the progress of regional integration initiatives in South America. Global economic relationships can enhance regional integration efforts by offering extra resources and collaboration opportunities. However, conflicting interests and geopolitical rivalry among external powers may hinder attempts to strengthen regional institutions and foster solidarity among South American nations.

7.Environmental and Social Impacts:

Infrastructure development projects linked to emerging economic alliances can have substantial environmental and social consequences, especially for indigenous communities and vulnerable ecosystems. South American countries must prioritize sustainable development techniques and ensure that economic growth benefits all parts of society while reducing negative environmental impacts.

The consequences of changing alliances and economic dynamics in South America are intricate and diverse. New partnerships present prospects for economic expansion and progress but also bring about difficulties concerning geopolitical rivalry, regional safety, political steadiness, and environmental durability. South American countries must manage these developments carefully, ensuring a delicate balance between national interests, regional collaboration, and sustainable development objectives.

The Future of South American Dynamics and Alliances

The geopolitical landscape in South America is complicated and ever-changing, with regional, global, and domestic variables all playing a role in shaping future alliances and dynamics. There are a number of possible future developments and trends that might affect the area's peace, prosperity, and diplomacy.

1. Uniting Regions vs. Separating Them

South American countries might become more economically and politically integrated to tackle shared problems and seize shared opportunities, which would be a significant step toward greater regional integration. Mercosur, the Pacific Alliance, and UNASUR are among the initiatives that might step up their game in encouraging cooperation and decreasing reliance on foreign powers. Yet, regional fragmentation and disunity could result from member nations' internal disagreements, conflicting interests, and ideological differences, which could impede attempts at further integration.

2. China's Growing Influence

As China strengthens its economic and geopolitical links with South American nations, its growing footprint in the area is expected to persist. Regional dynamics will be shaped by Chinese investments in energy, infrastructure, and natural resources, which could result in a greater reliance on China. Although these investments present chances for economic expansion, they also bring up worries over the long-term viability of debt, environmental damage, and social consequences.

3. U.S. Reengagement

Under new administrations, the U.S. may reestablish diplomatic relations with South American countries, aiming to fortify bonds with longstanding friends while reaching out to those seeking alliances with China and other international superpowers. The region's infrastructure development could receive more funding from initiatives such as Build Back Better World (B3W), part of the Biden administration. Skepticism and distrust stemming from previous interventions and contradictory policies may restrict the United States' capacity to reclaim influence.

4. Diversifying the Economy

There will be less reliance on commodities exports and less exposure to global market volatility if South American countries keep diversifying their economies. We can encourage economic diversification and foster sustainable growth by promoting innovation, entrepreneurship, and value-added businesses. Partnerships and regional trade agreements with developing economies in the Middle East, Africa, and Asia can open up new investment and market penetration avenues.

5. Difficulties with Security

South American countries will continue to face substantial problems when it comes to transnational security threats, including drug trafficking, organized crime, and illicit financial flows. Regional and international partners must enhance cooperation and intelligence-sharing to tackle these challenges effectively. Furthermore, territorial disputes and geopolitical rivalry can heighten tensions and derail regional security and peace attempts.

6. Sustainability in the Face of Climate Change

Extreme weather, deforestation, and biodiversity loss are ways South America is already feeling the effects of climate change. Sustainable land use methods, investments in renewable energy, conservation efforts, and global coordination are all necessary to meet these issues. To strengthen resilience, save ecosystems, and preserve livelihoods, working with international partners on climate adaptation and mitigation is essential.

Finally, it is not known what the future holds for the alliances and dynamics in South America. Growth and development prospects exist in regional integration, economic diversification, and cooperation with global powers. However, some risks and obstacles must be addressed via strategic planning, dialogue, and multilateral cooperation. If South American nations want to build a sustainable, prosperous, and peaceful future, they will need to negotiate these issues carefully.

Chapter 7: Western Democracies: Elections and Global Leadership

Impact on the world as a result of the Upcoming Elections in the United States

In several different ways, the election in the United States in 2024 has the potential to alter world leadership profoundly:

Alterations in the Global Dynamics:

1. America's Foreign Policy: It is possible for a dramatic shift in US foreign policy to occur due to a change in leadership. During their presidency, a Democratic president might emphasize multilateralism and working together with friends, whereas a Republican president might adopt a more unilateral approach. This has the potential to influence anything from commercial transactions to military operations.

2. The relationship with China: The competition between the United States and China is one of the defining characteristics of the 21st century. This vital relationship will be impacted by the new president's views on matters such as trade, human rights, and territorial disputes, among other things. A more aggressive strategy may cause tensions to rise, whereas a more cooperative approach may look for places where there is room for compromise.

3. International Organizations: In international institutions such as the United Nations and the North Atlantic Treaty Organization, the United States plays a crucial role. The effectiveness of these organizations in tackling global concerns could be diminished if the president is dubious of them.

Domestic Consequences and International Repercussions:

1. Economic Leadership: The United States dollar continues to be the reserve currency of the globe, and the economic policies of the United States have global repercussions. Global markets and financial stability are all influenced by various factors, including domestic spending, interest rates, and trade policy.

2. Military Power: America's military continues to be the most powerful in the world.

It is possible that global security dynamics could be affected by a president who prioritizes military spending or adopts a more assertive foreign policy. Allies could be encouraged by this, while competitors could become more resentful.

3. Populist Influence: A triumph for populists in the United States could spark similar movements worldwide, potentially leading to

an increase in nationalism and protectionism, further fracturing the existing order of the international community.

Various Potential Outcomes:

1.Continuity: If the approach taken by the current administration is maintained, the used States' foreign policy will likely be predictable. On the other hand, existing problems, such as climate change or the rise of China, will not be tackled with the appropriate level of urgency.

2.Populist Shift: A populist president might put "America First" policies at the forefront of his agenda, resulting in the weakening of alliances, the withdrawal from trade agreements, and the undermining of international participation. This may result in a global climate that is more unstable and unpredictable.

3.The Rebirth of Multilateralism: A president dedicated to multilateralism can rejuvenate international institutions and alliances, stimulating cooperation on issues affecting the world. This has the potential to result in a world order that is more stable and efficient.

Elections in the United States in 2024 will be a defining moment for global leadership. Depending on the outcome, the United States' attitude to the worldwide arena will be determined, which will have implications for everything from international collaboration to global security. The decisions that voters in the United States make will have significantly far-reaching repercussions, and the entire world is watching.

Global implications of the Upcoming elections in the UK

There is no doubt that the election in the United States has tremendous weight worldwide; nevertheless, the election in the United Kingdom also has the potential to alter international leadership, albeit more subtly dramatically. In this manner:

The UK's Shrinking Stage, But Enduring Influence:

Post-Brexit Britain: The United Kingdom's influence on the international stage has decreased since it left the European Union.

Despite this, it continues to exert a significant military presence and has a permanent seat on the United Nations Security Council. The election's outcome may decide how efficiently the United Kingdom uses the authority it still possesses.

Aims of the "Global Britain" Strategy: Some people in the United Kingdom support the concept of "Global Britain" as a plan for preserving the country's influence beyond the borders of Europe. The commitment of the chosen leader to this goal will define the role that the United Kingdom plays in international affairs.

The influence on the Western World and the established order of the world:

Relationship with the United States of America: The alliance between the United Kingdom and the United States is a fundamental component of the Western system. The elected leader's position on whether or not to work with the United States on global problems such as trade and security can affect the Western world's collective power.

1. Leadership in the Commonwealth: The United Kingdom is the leader of the Commonwealth of Nations, comprised of formerly British colonies. How the leader approaches this connection has the potential to impact international commerce and development, particularly in Africa.

2. International Norms and the Concept of Soft Power: Throughout history, the United Kingdom has proudly advocated for democracy, human rights, and the rule of law. The dedication of the elected leader to these ideals has the potential to influence the global community's agenda and inspire other nations.

Situations That Could Occur

i. Consistency and a pragmatic approach: The traditional role of the United Kingdom as a bridge between Europe and North America might be preserved if the country's leader prioritizes maintaining a stable relationship with the United States and continuing to work together on global concerns.

ii. Inward Focus: Putting domestic matters first might cause a leader to overlook foreign engagement, reducing the United Kingdom's influence on the world stage. Polly could cause the Western alliance to become more fractured.

iii. The push for "Global Britain": Under the leadership of a person dedicated to the "Global Britain" vision, new trade ties and relationships with developing countries might be formed, potentially reshaping the existing order in the world.

Although the election in the United Kingdom is not as much of a worldwide spectacle as the election in the United States, the outcome of the election will impact how the United Kingdom interacts with the rest of the globe. Consequently, this affects the efficiency of the Western World as well as the overall stability of the international order.

USA and UK's Elections potential impact on International Relations

There are several ways in which the impending elections in the United States of America and the United Kingdom have the potential to alter international relations significantly:

"The Special Relationship" between the United States and the United Kingdom:

Both countries' leadership styles have the potential to have an impact on the degree of cooperation that exists between them. A strong relationship between the United States of America and the United Kingdom is frequently referred to as a "special relationship," It benefits both countries in terms of trade and defense. There is the potential for this tie to be strained when presidents have personality problems or disagreements regarding foreign policy.

Global Issues:

International cooperation is required to effectively address issues such as the containment of China, the ongoing conflict in Ukraine, and the solutions to climate change. The strategies favored by the governments of the United States and the United Kingdom can affect how effectively the globe addresses these difficulties.

European Security:

For a long time, the United States has been a significant player in the security of Europe. Assuming that a new leader in the United States was to adopt a more isolationist stance, this could increase the pressure placed on European states to strengthen their defenses. Another factor contributing to this is the connection the United Kingdom will have with the European Union once it leaves the EU.

It is essential to remember that the implications above are merely prospective outcomes; the actual result will be determined by the particular politicians who emerge victorious in the elections and their policy positions.

Chapter 8: The Erosion of Democracy under Trump, Putin, and Other Power-Hungry Leaders

The deterioration of democracy under the leadership of individuals such as Trump, Putin, and others is a phenomenon that is intricate and multi-faceted, and it calls for an in-depth investigation into the many different variables and dynamics that are at play.

This erosion manifests itself in various ways depending on the setting. Still, some of the present common themes include attacks on democratic institutions, a weakening of the rule of law, an erosion of civil freedoms, manipulation of the media, and a consolidation of power in the hands of the ruling class. As part of this in-depth research, we will investigate the specific techniques that these leaders have utilized, as well as the historical and sociopolitical conditions that have enabled their ascent to power, and we will also discuss the implications of these strategies for democracy and global governance.

How Leaders Are Posing a Risk to Democratic Institutions

The deterioration of democracy that has occurred under the leadership of individuals such as Donald Trump in the United States and Vladimir Putin in Russia poses a fundamental challenge to the ideals that serve as the foundation of liberal democracy. The leaders in question and others characterized as "hungry for power" have employed various strategies to weaken democratic norms and institutions, consolidating their influence and ensuring that they continue to rule. To evaluate the current status of global governance and plot a course for its future, it is essential to have a solid understanding of the mechanisms responsible for the erosion of democracy from the inside.

Democracy context

It is vital to consider the historical context in which leaders such as Trump and Putin came into existence to comprehend the deterioration of democracy that they have caused. Many political turmoil and transitions have occurred in the United States of America and Russia over the last few decades.

For the United States of America, the conclusion of the Cold War signaled the beginning of a period characterized by relative stability and prosperity. Nevertheless, the 21st century has witnessed increasing polarization, which has exacerbated economic disparity, cultural divides, and the growth of identity politics. The election of Donald Trump in 2016 was a culmination of these tendencies, with his populist rhetoric and unusual political style resonating with dissatisfied portions of the population. This election was a result of Trump's election.

Similarly, Russia underwent significant transformations after the fall of the Soviet Union; during the transition from communism to capitalism, economic upheaval and social transition co-occurred. After several years of anarchy and decay, Vladimir Putin emerged as a strongman leader, promising stability and national regeneration before departing from power. On the other hand, his rule has been marked by authoritarian inclinations and crackdowns on political dissent by the government.

Erosion strategies and tactics:

Legal, political, and rhetorical techniques are being utilized to consolidate power and stifle opposition to bring about the loss of democracy that is taking place under the leadership of leaders such as Trump and Putin. Among these types of strategies are:

Attacks on Democratic Institutions Leaders are responsible for undermining the independence and integrity of democratic institutions such as the legislature, the judiciary, and the media. Appointing loyalists to crucial positions, attacking the legitimacy of institutions held by the opposition, and attempting to delegitimize the democratic process are all practices that can fall under this category.

Deterioration of the Rule of Law:

By selectively applying legal norms to target political opponents while insulating themselves and their allies from accountability, leaders undermine the rule of law and the rule of law itself. The politicization of law enforcement agencies, the manipulation of the legal system, and the passage of legislation restricting civil freedoms under the pretense of national security or public order are all strategies that might be utilized to accomplish this.

The deterioration of democratic rights:

Leaders impose restrictions on the rights to freedom of expression, assembly, and association to stifle dissent and preserve their authority over the public. Censorship of critical media outlets, harassment of political activists, and the passage of legislation that penalizes peaceful protest or dissenting perspectives are all examples of actions that can be taken in this context.

The Act of Manipulating the Media:

Leaders utilize media channels controlled by the state or considered supportive of distributing propaganda and disinformation to manipulate public opinion in their favor and marginalize competing narratives. This can include directly restricting or intimidating journalists who dispute the official narrative and co-opting commercial media businesses through regulatory capture or economic incentives. Additionally, this can involve either of these two methods.

Increased Concentration of Power:

To marginalize competing factions within the governing elite and neutralize possible rivals, leaders concentrate power in their own hands and those in their inner circle where they are surrounded. It is possible to accomplish this by removing disloyal officials from their positions, consolidating decision-making procedures, and modifying constitutions or electoral rules to ensure their reign is maintained indefinitely.

Studies of Trump and Putin as Case Studies

Let's take a look at the deterioration of democracy that has occurred under the leadership of Donald Trump in the United States and Vladimir Putin in Russia as an example of how these techniques might be put into effect.

a) Donald Trump

While serving as President of the United States, Donald Trump utilized a wide range of strategies to undermine democratic norms and institutions for the duration of his presidency. In addition to these,

Attempts to Assault the Media:

On numerous occasions, Trump referred to journalists and media outlets that were critical of his administration as "fake news" and stated that they were "the enemy of the people." He intended to destroy public trust in the press and delegitimize negative coverage to diminish the press's capacity to hold him accountable legally.

Compromises with the Judicial System:

There were disagreements between Trump and the judicial system about subjects such as his controversial travel ban that targeted countries that were primarily Muslim. He challenged the separation of powers and the notion of judicial independence by calling into question the impartiality and legitimacy of judges who issued decisions contrary to his policies.

The application of politics to law enforcement:

Several law enforcement agencies, including the Department of Justice and the Federal Bureau of Investigation, were accused of being politicized by Trump. Through his efforts to exert control over investigations into his behavior, as well as the behavior of his friends, he attempted to throw doubt on the impartiality and integrity of the criminal justice system.

Disintegration of Norms:

The norms and institutions of democracy have been further weakened due to Trump's actions, which violate established rules of presidential conduct and disregard those principles. His refusal to reveal his tax returns, his use of executive orders to circumvent Congress, and the conflicts of interest that stemmed from his corporate empire all undermined the values of transparency and accountability.

b) Vladimir Putin.

Vladimir Putin has been responsible for the gradual decline of democracy in Russia, which he has accomplished through a combination of authoritarian policies and the manipulation of the political system. Techniques that he has used include:

Having Command of the Media:

The Russian media landscape has been consolidated under Putin's control, which has resulted in the silencing of critical voices and the monopolization of the distribution of information. Television channels that are owned by the state and outlets that are supportive of the government dominate the airwaves, while independent journalists are subjected to intimidation, censorship, and even physical violence.

Repression of an Oppositional Political Personnel:

Systematically, Putin has marginalized political opposition parties and people by employing both legal and extralegal tactics. The state is responsible for orchestrating smear campaigns, causing opposition leaders to be subjected to arbitrary arrests and making up charges against them. Elections are highly controlled to guarantee that Putin's United Russia party would continue to have most seats.

Centralization of Power:

The power of the presidency has been consolidated under Putin's leadership, which has resulted in the weakening of other parts of government and the erosion of checks and balances. He modified the Russian constitution to extend his rule, which included the elimination of term restrictions and the allocation of extensive administrative powers to himself. As a result of the Kremlin's grip over regional governors and local administrations, the autonomy of subnational institutions is further diminished.

Repression of Civic Organizations:

Those regarded as threatening to Putin's authority include civil society organizations, human rights advocates, and independent nongovernmental organizations (NGOs). They are subject to rigorous government scrutiny, their actions are restricted by draconian legislation, and they must comply with excessive reporting requirements. NGOs that receive funding from other countries are referred to as "foreign agents" and are exposed to harassment and intimidation.

Global Implications

The deterioration of democracy carried out by leaders such as Trump and Putin have substantial repercussions for the world's governance and the international community's established order. These include the following:

A Deterioration of Norms:

The normative foundation of liberal democracy around the world is being undermined by the decline of democracy in states that have significant influence. The moral authority of democratic powers to promote human rights and democratic government globally is undermined, and authoritarian regimes are given more confidence.

The instability of the region:

There is a correlation between the consolidation of power in the hands of authoritarian leaders and the escalation of conflict and instability in the region. There is a greater likelihood that authoritarian regimes will resort to coercion and military force to maintain power, exacerbating existing tensions and generating insecurity. Autocratic regimes are also less sensitive to the complaints of their subjects.

A Disruption to the Economy:

Because it affects the rule of law, property rights, and the execution of contracts, the erosion of democracy can cause disruptions to economic stability and inhibit progress. Investors may perceive authoritarian regimes as hazardous and unpredictable, which can result in the flight of capital and a reduction in investment flows inside the country.

The fall of the Democratic Party:

There is the potential for the degradation of democracy in one nation to create a domino effect, which can inspire similar authoritarian impulses in surrounding states or embolden authoritarian leaders in other countries. This can potentially contribute to a more widespread trend of democratic regression and the weakening of liberal norms worldwide. The values of liberal democracy and the rule of law are being put to the test in a significant way by the deterioration of democracy that is taking place under the leadership of leaders such as Trump, Putin, and others who are eager for power. To consolidate their control and maintain their rule, these leaders employ various measures, including legal, political, and rhetorical tactics, to destroy democratic institutions, erode the rule of law, and repress political opposition.

To combat this erosion, civil society, political actors, and international organizations must work together to safeguard democratic norms and institutions, uphold the rule of law, and promote human rights and democratic governance worldwide. It is only by confrontation with authoritarianism and the reaffirmation of the values of democracy and freedom that we can have any hope of protecting the future of democracy in a world that is becoming increasingly uncertain.

How presidents and other national leaders exercise their powers beyond the mandates of the Constitution

When expanding their authority beyond the limitations set by the Constitution, presidents and other national leaders frequently resort to various methods. This is especially true for those with authoritarian tendencies or a craving for strength. Even though constitutions commonly describe the powers and restrictions of executive authority, leaders may take advantage of gaps, manipulate legal frameworks, or flout established standards to consolidate power and exert control. The following is a list of the various ways in which presidents and other leading national figures may violate their constitutional rights:

Executive Orders and Decrees:

Presidents and other heads of state can issue executive orders or decrees by many constitutions. These orders or decrees carry the same weight as laws and do not require legislative approval. Leaders can abuse these instruments to sidestep the legislative process and unilaterally impose their agenda, even though they are designed to be used in unexpected situations or to implement laws already in place. The principle of separation of powers may be undermined due to this possibility, which can lead to the concentration of power in the hands of the executive branch.

Manipulation of Legal Systems

There is a possibility that presidents and other national leaders will attempt to abuse legal institutions to protect themselves from accountability or to target political opponents. The appointment of loyalists to crucial posts within the court, the intimidation of judges or prosecutors, and the passage of legislation that offers immunity to particular individuals or actions all fall under this category. It is possible for leaders to avoid being subjected to judicial examination and solidify their dominance without being challenged if they co-opt or undermine the court's independence.

Expanding the number of emergency powers:

In times of crisis, constitutions frequently include provisions that allow for the proclamation of a state of emergency. This gives the executive branch additional authority to respond to the situation effectively. It is possible, however, for authorities to use these laws to prolong emergency measures indefinitely, restrict civil liberties, and repress opposing voices. Under the idea of preserving stability or national security, emergency powers can provide authoritarian leaders with a pretext to consolidate authority, suppress opposition, and continue to reign under the cover of sustaining stability.

Use of Security Forces and Paramilitary Groups:

For intimidating political opponents, suppressing protests, or enforcing their will, presidents and other national leaders may utilize security forces, intelligence agencies, or paramilitary groups. Arrests made without due process of law, extrajudicial killings, or the use of force against civilians are all examples of this type of behavior, which undermines the rule of law and civil freedoms. The ability to monopolize the tools of violence and scare dissenters into submission can be achieved by leaders through the co-optation or coercion of security forces.

Control of the Information and Media World:

Through propaganda, censorship, or state-controlled media, people in positions of authority may attempt to control the flow of information and shape public opinion. Those in positions of authority can mold public perceptions and strengthen their hold on power by stifling voices of dissent, spreading disinformation, or demonizing politically opposed individuals. The suppression of criticism and the maintenance of control over the narrative are frequent strategies utilized. These strategies include the censorship of social media, the harassment of journalists, and restrictions on the freedom of the press.

Manipulation of Electoral Processes:

Presidents and other national leaders can manipulate electoral processes while simultaneously undermining the legitimacy of democratic institutions to maintain their continuing domination. Gerrymandering, voter suppression, tampering with election results, and harassing opposition candidates and supporters are all examples of political activities that fall under this category. The ability of leaders to maintain their dominance and stifle alternative voices inside the political system can be achieved through the manipulation of elections or by tilting the playing field in their own favor.

Amendment of Constitutions:

As a means of consolidating their control and weakening the checks and balances that are in place to protect executive power, leaders may attempt to change or revise constitutions. The expansion of presidential terms, the elimination of term limits, and the concentration of decision-making authority in the hands of the executive branch are all potential solutions to this problem. Legal processes that allow for the modification of constitutional frameworks can be utilized by leaders to firmly establish their rules and avoid being held accountable for their acts.

In general, presidents and other national leaders can go beyond the constitutional rights they are granted by taking advantage of legal gaps, manipulating institutions, and disrespecting democratic regulations. Because this erosion of constitutional limits on executive authority poses a significant threat to the principles of democracy, rule of law, and human rights, civil society, political opposition, and international actors must exercise vigilant oversight and resistance to protect democratic governance and accountability.

Is it possible for leaders who are corrupt and greedy to avoid being arrested or having any action taken against them?

Corrupt and greedy politicians frequently resort to various strategies to avoid being arrested and keep their hold on power. These strategies include the manipulation of legal systems, the intimidation of political opponents and law enforcement agencies, and the control of security personnel. Some individuals may use paramilitary forces or militia groups to safeguard themselves; however, this is not always the case, and other techniques may also be utilized. One can avoid being arrested by several different methods, including the following:

Control over the Legal Systems:

To avoid being held accountable for their actions, corrupt officials may attempt to manipulate or co-opt legal systems. This may involve the appointment of loyalists to crucial court positions, the intimidation of judges or prosecutors, or the passage of legislation that offers immunity to particular individuals or conduct. Effectively dodging arrest and prosecution, leaders can prevent or prolong investigations, trials, and convictions by exerting influence over the judicial system. This allows them to avoid being arrested and prosecuted.

Harassment and intimidation of those who are in opposition:

Political opponents, campaigners, and whistleblowers who threaten corrupt leaders' interests are frequently subjected to intimidation and harassment measures by these leaders. Security forces or loyalist groups can coordinate harassment campaigns, physical violence, arbitrary arrests, and fabricated charges. Other examples include threats of bodily harm. The ability to generate fear and silence dissent is a powerful tool that leaders can use to discourage criticism and avoid taking responsibility for their actions.

Taking Command of the Security Forces:

Corrupt leaders can maintain influence over security forces, intelligence agencies, or paramilitary groups to protect themselves from arrest and oppress anyone who disagrees with them. Intimidation or coercion of law enforcement authorities, obstruction of investigations, and suppression of demonstrations and uprisings are all possible utilizations of these forces. Leaders can preserve their hold on power and resist attempts to hold them accountable by monopolizing the instruments of violence.

The Influence of Politicians and the Networks of Patronage:

Leaders who engage in corrupt practices frequently construct vast networks consisting of political supporters, commercial partners, and patronage benefactors who provide them with support and protection. Due to the fact that these networks can give financial support, legal assistance, and political cover, it becomes more difficult for law enforcement agencies to pursue investigations or enforce arrest warrants. Leaders can protect themselves from prosecution and continue to enjoy impunity if they cultivate loyalty and reward loyalty.

The provision of diplomatic immunity and international support:

Corrupt leaders can seek refuge in foreign countries that are willing to grant asylum or protection from arrest and extradition. Utilizing diplomatic links, using personal connections with foreign leaders, or getting asylum through political or humanitarian routes are all examples of ways that this might be accomplished. Furthermore, leaders may strive to secure diplomatic immunity by holding official positions in international organizations or by participating in diplomatic operations. This offers them the opportunity to effectively insulate themselves from legal accountability.

The use of Proxy Actors:

In certain instances, corrupt leaders may use proxy actors, such as militia organizations or private security contractors, to shield themselves from arrest and quell opposition. There is a possibility that these groups will be assigned the responsibility of providing physical protection, conducting surveillance, or carrying out violent retaliation against perceived threats. When leaders outsource the use of coercion and violence to proxy actors, they can remove themselves from direct involvement while still keeping control over their security apparatus.

In general, corrupt and greedy leaders use a variety of strategies to avoid being arrested and to keep their power. These strategies include the manipulation of judicial systems, the intimidation of opponents, the control of security forces, and the utilization of international support. Even if some people may turn to organizing paramilitary forces or militia organizations, alternative techniques may be just as effective in preserving their interests and maintaining their impunity. To overcome the obstacles posed by entrenched authoritarian regimes and kleptocratic elites, it is necessary to have powerful legal frameworks, independent institutions, and international collaboration to address corruption and hold leaders accountable.

The question is whether or not any actions are being taken against greedy leaders such as Putin and Trump, who obstruct democracy.

It is necessary to conduct a comprehensive analysis of local and international responses to address the actions that have been taken against leaders such as Putin and Trump, who are regarded as weakening democracy. The amount to which concrete measures have been taken against these leaders varies depending on the strength of democratic institutions, political dynamics, and international relations. Even though these leaders have been criticized and resisted for their acts, more concrete measures have been taken against them. The following section will discuss the steps taken against such leaders, particularly on global and domestic initiatives.

•Responses from Domestic or Individual Country Legal Challenges and Investigations:

Leaders who undermine democracy may be subject to legal challenges and investigations in countries that are democratic and have robust judicial systems. As an illustration, in the case of Donald Trump, several legal cases have been brought against him on multiple occasions, both during his presidency and after it ended. Among them are inquiries into possible instances of obstructing the administration of justice, fraudulent financial practices, and authority violations. Even though President Trump was not charged with any crimes, the investigation that Special Counsel Robert Mueller conducted into Russian meddling in the 2016 election resulted in several indictments and convictions.

To a similar extent, in Russia, opposition politicians and civil society organizations have attempted to hold Putin accountable through legal channels despite encountering substantial difficulties and repression. Even though Navalny, a renowned leader of the Russian opposition, has been arrested and imprisoned on multiple occasions for his activity, his Anti-wrongdoing Foundation continues to expose wrongdoing inside the government and collect support from the general people.

Political Opposition and Protests:

In nations with a robust political opposition movement, leaders who delay the implementation of democracy may be subjected to persistent pressure from opposition parties and civil society organizations. The presidency of Donald Trump in the United States spurred extensive protests and mobilization, particularly among progressive activists and communities who have been excluded. To bring attention to issues such as racism, sexism, and authoritarianism, numerous organizations, including the Women's March, Black Lives Matter, and Indivisible, planned large-scale rallies in opposition to the policies and rhetoric of current President Donald Trump.

In a similar vein, opposition individuals in Russia, such as Navalny, have successfully rallied popular support through grassroots organizing and social media engagement despite the significant restrictions placed on political dissent and freedom of assembly. Even though Russian authorities have been arresting and violently cracking down on protesters, thousands of people have shown their support for Navalny's calls for anti- corruption demonstrations.

Accountability for the Elections:

Leaders that undermine democracy in democratic nations may be subject to electoral consequences if people hold them accountable for their acts for the consequences of their actions. In the case of Donald Trump, his loss in the presidential election 2020 was widely interpreted as a criticism of the policies and actions taken by his administration, particularly his management of the COVID-19 pandemic and his efforts to change the election results. In the face of an effort at authoritarianism, democratic institutions demonstrated their durability through the peaceful transition of power to President Joe Biden.

Similar to the situation in the United States, opposition candidates in Russia have successfully won local and regional elections in some instances despite extensive charges of electoral fraud and manipulation. This is evidence of the widespread dissatisfaction with Putin's administration. On the other hand, opposition parties have a difficult time competing on a fair playing field because the Kremlin maintains control over the electoral process and the media.

•International Responses:

Diplomatic Pressure and Sanctions:

Diplomatic pressure and penalties may be applied by other nations and international organizations on leaders who delay the implementation of democratic principles on the world stage. The annexation of Crimea by Russia, as well as Russia's involvement in crises in Ukraine and Syria, have led to economic sanctions and diplomatic isolation from the United States of America, the European Union, and other Western nations. This is the situation with Putin. Some of the most critical sectors of the Russian economy, as well as persons and organizations with close ties to the Kremlin, are the specific targets of these sanctions.

In a similar vein, the administration of Donald Trump has strained relations between the United States of America and its allies, notably about disputes about trade, climate change, and NATO. The warm and intimate relationship that President Trump has with authoritarian leaders such as Vladimir Putin and Kim Jong-un of North Korea has caused Western democracies to express alarm regarding the deterioration of democratic norms and principles on the international scene.

Support for Civil Society and Democratic Institutions:

International organizations and civil society groups play a significant role in ensuring the protection of human rights and democratic principles in nations facing challenges to these principles. Civil society organizations, independent media outlets, and democratic institutions in countries such as the United States and Russia get financial support, technical aid, and advocacy support from organizations such as the United Nations, the European Union, and non-governmental organizations (NGOs) that focus on human rights.

In the case of Russia, for instance, international groups such as Human Rights Watch and Amnesty International have recorded violations of human rights and lobbied for the release of political prisoners such as Navalny. A similar pattern has been observed in the United States, where non-governmental organizations (NGOs) like the American Civil Liberties Union (ACLU) have initiated legal actions to challenge the Trump administration's policies regarding matters such as freedom of speech, LGBTQ rights, and immigration.

In conclusion, efforts are being taken against leaders such as Putin and Trump that defer democracy domestically and internationally. These actions are being taken. Leaders who undermine democracy can be held accountable for their activities through various measures, including but not limited to legal challenges, political opposition, electoral accountability, diplomatic pressure, and support for civil society. On the other hand, the effectiveness of these efforts is contingent upon a wide range of circumstances, such as the robustness of democratic institutions, the resiliency of civil society, and the willingness of other nations to defend democratic norms on the international stage. In the end, maintaining continued attention and participation from individuals, activists, and governments worldwide is necessary to protect democracy.

The Erosion of Democracy: A Detrimental Impact on Common People

For those seeking representation, equality, and fairness, democracy—often regarded as society's apex—bears hope. However, a dangerous reality lurks beneath its surface: democracies are being threatened. The very fabric of our democratic system is eroding, with authoritarianism and civil rights both making steady inroads. The effects of this weakening of democratic values are widespread and disproportionately felt by the average citizen. We look at the ways that everyday people's lives are negatively impacted by the decline of democracy in this essay.

Political Apathy and Disenfranchisement:

The trust of the general public in government declines in tandem with the decline of democracy. Disenfranchisement is a result of gerrymandering, the practice of suppressing the vote, and the power of money in politics. People lose faith in government and stop caring about making a difference when they believe their votes don't matter or that the system is biased against them. Ordinary folks are rendered voiceless and excluded as a result of this political disengagement, which further solidifies current power systems.

Social Discontent and Economic Inequality:

The World in Turmoil

Increasing economic disparity is frequently associated with the weakening of democracies. When democratic institutions deteriorate, the powerful and rich have their way at the expense of the common people. Common people are already struggling to make ends meet, and policies that support deregulation, tax cuts for the wealthy, and austerity measures just make things worse. As a result of bearing a disproportionate share of the costs associated with inequality, economically disenfranchised populations are more likely to experience anger and social violence.

Dangers to Individual Freedoms and Human Rights:

It is common practice to prioritize national security and stability over civil liberties and human rights when democracies are weakening. Censorship, crackdowns on dissent, and surveillance all make ordinary people more susceptible to abuse by totalitarian governments. Activists, journalists, and members of minority groups face extra-judicial persecution in the form of threats, arrest, or worse for voicing their opposition to injustice. An environment of terror and tyranny is fostered when civil rights are eroded, which has the dual effect of reducing personal autonomy and weakening democracy itself.

Social Discord and Polarization:

Eroding democratic standards frequently promotes polarization and societal division, which contradicts the ideal of inclusivity upon which democracies are based. In order to consolidate power, political leaders use identity politics, which incites fear and animosity, to create a "us vs. them" attitude that breaks down social cohesiveness. The common people are divided along ideological, religious, or racial lines, which serves to deflect criticism from larger structural problems and to keep people hostile toward one another. Further undermining the democratic process, a climate of polarization makes it harder than ever to have fruitful conversations and find common ground.

Infrastructure and Public Services in Decline:

Public services and infrastructure go down the drain when democratic institutions go down the drain. Mismanagement of healthcare, education, and transportation occurs as a result of government agencies' lack of accountability, inefficiency, and corruption. Overcrowded schools, poor healthcare, and decaying infrastructure are some of the ways that the average person feels the effects of these failures. Deterioration of democracy has far-reaching consequences, including worsening living conditions for average residents and feeding the vicious cycle of poverty and inequality.

The rights, liberties, and welfare of the common people are jeopardized as a result of democracy's decline. The ramifications of democratic disintegration are far-reaching and negative, ranging from economic disparity and social discontent to disenfranchisement and political indifference. In order to protect democracy and make sure everyone has a fair shot at the future, we need to get to the bottom of why democracies are crumbling, make the powerful answer for their actions, and give regular people a voice in politics. We can only reverse the trend of decline and create a more equitable and welcoming society for future generations if we work together and recommit to democratic values.

Conclusion

World wars and conflicts cause chaos and stress on a global scale, showing up as economic instability, humanitarian crises, and rifts in politics. These wars make countries distrust each other, which makes it harder to negotiate and keeps violence going. In addition, they make social differences worse, spread extremist ideas, and make it harder for countries to work together. The results are felt across borders, causing trade problems, forcing millions of people to move, and threatening human rights. To solve these problems, we need coordinated diplomatic, humanitarian, and economic efforts. To keep the peace that was started, people must be willing to talk to each other, work out their differences, and try to understand each other better for the peace to last.

When Russia took over Crimea and sent troops into eastern Ukraine, it caused major geopolitical problems. Western countries condemned Russia's actions and put sanctions on it, but Russia saw these actions as interference in its area of influence and rejected them. This has made things difficult between Russia and the West, adding to an environment of mistrust and competition in general. In the same way, the conflict between Israel and Hamas has made things worse between people in the area and around the world. The repeated fighting between Israel and Hamas makes Palestinians angrier and more frustrated, which causes large-scale protests and unrest in the area. It causes arguments about Israel's security measures and Palestinian rights on a global level, and it gets support from Iran and the US, which splits views and causes diplomatic problems. China's rise has had a huge impact on the world, changing the economic, political, and military landscapes of countries in the South China Sea, such as China, Malaysia, Vietnam, the Philippines, Brunei, and Taiwan. It poses a threat to traditional economic powerhouses and is changing the way trade and business happen around the world. In terms of politics, it shows its power through projects like the Belt and Road, which change the way geopolitics works. From a strategic point of view, it changes the rules for security, which makes competition stronger in key areas like the South China Sea. In the United States, it makes people want to modernize and worry about dictatorship. Culturally, it boosts China's "soft power" around the world. China's rise presents both opportunities and challenges, necessitating the complex handling of diplomacy, trade, and government to effectively manage its effects.

The trade disputes between the United States and China have caused major economic problems and had effects all over the world. Trade has been slowed down by tariffs and retaliatory measures, which hurts both companies and consumers. Supply chains have changed, and businesses all over the world are feeling the effects of higher costs and less certainty. There have been problems in diplomatic ties, which has made geopolitical tensions worse and caused worries about a wider economic decoupling. Even though talks have happened, it is still hard to find long-lasting answers. The disagreements have shown that global trade has fundamental problems and led to calls for change. To deal with these tensions, we need to have strategic conversations, trade fairly, and work together to find answers that hurt economies and relations between countries.

The Indian political scene offers both problems and chances for the country's economy. Problems include inefficient government agencies, complicated rules, and unstable governments that make it hard for businesses to spend and grow. Corruption and social unrest are also big problems that make it hard to grow. On the other hand, India's large market, young population, and growing middle class present huge opportunities for economic growth. India has the ability to become a global economic powerhouse if it makes changes to improve infrastructure, make rules easier to understand, and encourage new ideas. Efforts to improve relations with other countries through diplomacy also make trade and business possible. To get around India's complicated landscape and live up to its potential as a dynamic economic force, it is important to find a balance between political stability, inclusive government, and long-term economic policies.

Pakistan's elections and economic problems are intertwined and have an impact on the country's future. During the election process, there is political division, instability, and claims of wrongdoing, which slows down democracy's progress. High inflation, unemployment, and a dependence on foreign aid are all problems with the economy that make it hard for people to get along and support each other. Many factors, including its ties with countries like the US, China, India, and those in the eastern Mediterranean Sea, influence Pakistan's economy. Pakistan's growth is affected by its economic ties with the US, which include trade, investment, and foreign help. When the US gives Pakistan money, it often comes with rules about human rights, security, and government. These rules affect Pakistan's policies. Trade relations affect Pakistan's economic growth and stability by affecting what it sells, what it imports, and how easy it is to get to markets. Investments from the United States in Pakistan's science, energy, and infrastructure can also help the country grow. Changes in US policy or geopolitical tensions, however, could break these links, which would hurt Pakistan's economy. So, keeping good diplomatic ties and building partnerships that are good for both sides are very important for Pakistan's economic health.

Changes in South America; particularly Brazil and Mexico, affect the world as a whole and make things more tense. As a regional powerhouse, Brazil has an impact on trade, environmental laws, and the stability of the region. Its changes in government and economy can mess up markets and investment flows around the world. Brazil's views on topics like climate change and cutting down trees also have an impact on efforts to work together for sustainability and international cooperation. Because it is so close to the US, Mexico is very important to trade and immigration laws in North America. If Mexico's government or trade ties with the US change, it can have an effect on supply chains and the world economy as a whole. Changes in both countries, like new leaders, trade policies, or regional allies, can make things uncertain and raise geopolitical tensions. Tensions are made worse by the fact that different world powers want to have an impact on South America. To promote security and cooperation on the world stage, it is important to understand and control the changing dynamics in Brazil, Mexico, and the rest of South America.

Due to changing geopolitical alignments and struggles for power, the growth of new partnerships in South America could lead to tensions around the world. As countries in South America try to expand their foreign relationships beyond their traditional allies, they may join forces with new powers like China and Russia or regional groups like the Pacific Alliance. Globally, new relationships in South America could lead to power struggles and economic growth, but they could also cause tensions and conflicts in world politics. To ease these tensions and encourage cooperation for the good of everyone, it will be important to use good diplomacy and conversation.

Similarly, the future elections in the United States will have big effects on the rest of the world. To begin, they will have an effect on trade, business, and financial markets around the world by shaping global economic policies and trends. Second, changes in U.S. foreign policy under new leadership could affect security arrangements, international partnerships, and how the world deals with problems like terrorism and climate change. Third, the elections will have an effect on diplomatic ties, which will have an effect on conflicts and cooperation in places like Europe, the Middle East, and the Asia-Pacific. The results could also change the international order by affecting global organizations and multilateral agreements. The elections will also set examples for democracy and government, which will have an effect on political groups and norms around the world. The results of the

U.S. elections will have an impact on politics, the economy, and international relations for many years to come.

Finally, leaders like Trump, Putin, and others are destroying democracy by attacking democratic structures, silencing dissent, and making power stronger. The way Trump talks about the media, attacks on the courts, and tries to mess up the election process have all hurt democratic values in the US. Putin's authoritarian tendencies have similarly hindered political opponents from winning elections, curtailed civil freedoms, and prevented independent media from operating in Russia. The future of democracy doesn't look good with these kinds of politicians in charge. Breaking down democratic ideals repeatedly puts freedoms, human rights, and the rule of law in danger. Misinformation and polarization feed populist goals, which split societies and make people less trusting of democratic institutions. But resilience comes from civil society, action at the local level, and working together across borders. To uphold democratic ideals, we need strong institutions, open government, and involved citizens. Dealing with the problems that power-hungry leaders cause requires a strong dedication to protecting democracy and encouraging responsibility at all levels of society.

Chapter 9: The current Shocking Twists in U.S. Politics: Assassination Attempt on Trump and Biden's Unexpected Exit from the Presidential Race"

Trump's assassination plot

Donald Trump, former US president and Republican Party presumptive presidential nominee in 2024, survived an assassination attempt while speaking at a campaign rally near Butler, Pennsylvania, on July 13, 2024. Trump sustained gunshot wounds to the top right ear. [6] A 20-year-old man named Thomas Matthew Crooks from Bethel Park, Pennsylvania, shot eight rounds from a building's rooftop, which was located 400 feet (120 meters) away from the stage. The criminals also critically wounded two additional audience members and murdered Corey Cooper. The United States Secret Service's Counter Sniper Team later shot and killed Crooks. The event took place while

Donald Trump was already widely expected to be the Republican presidential nominee for 2024. Two days prior to the 2024 Republican National Convention's start in Milwaukee, Wisconsin, on July 15, the shooting took place. A man tried to seize a security guard's gun at a Trump rally outside of Las Vegas in 2016, marking the first violent incident involving one of his rallies. If we examine how the incident occurred, we can better understand it.

What occurred during the assassination attempt on Trump?

An announcement on July 3, 2024, stated that Trump planned to hold a rally near Butler, Pennsylvania, in Connoquenessing Township and Meridian. An advance crew set up generators in a wide open field on July 10 to prepare for the rally. Pennsylvania has 19 electoral college votes, making it a potentially pivotal state for the Trump campaign. The rally was part of their Keystone State voter outreach. The rally featured an invitation to Republican candidate David McCormick, who is running for U.S. Senate in the state at the same time, to come onstage and garner more support for his campaign. The Trump campaign reportedly told U.S. Representative Mike Kelly, "We appreciate your input, but we've already made up our minds," when Kelly asked them to reconsider using the Butler Farm Show Grounds as the site of the rally, citing capacity concerns. Everyone who wants to attend a Trump rally must go through security, which includes a search for weapons. The Secret Service routinely screens and monitors nearby buildings and businesses, even those outside of security perimeters. State police patrolled one outer area, while Secret Service agents manned the inner perimeter as part of the event's security measures. In addition, the Secret Service and local law enforcement each sent two counter-sniper teams to the event. The Pennsylvania State Police, who are the local cops in Connoquenessing Township, were also involved in safety concerns. The Butler Township police took on the traffic duties. Prior to the incident, the FBI had no knowledge of any specific dangers. The Secret Service had already beefed up Trump's security detail in earlier weeks due to intelligence suggesting that Iran was attempting to assassinate him. The Iranian Foreign Minister refuted that assertion.

The shooting:

On July 7, 2024, Crooks visited the Butler Farm Show grounds, the site of Trump's campaign rally announced four days earlier. He signed up to attend the rally after spending twenty minutes there. On July 12, Crooks visited a shooting range to hone his skills with his rifle, inherited from his father and manufactured by DPMS Panther Arms. The rifle, chambered in 5.56mm NATO, boasted a 16-inch (41 cm) barrel.

Thomas Matthew Crooks purchased a five-foot (1.5-meter) ladder on July 13, the day of the assassination attempt, and then drove to the rally site in the morning. After leaving the rally site, he went to a gun store and purchased 50 rounds of ammunition. At 3:35 p.m. EDT, he returned to the rally with his rifle and an explosive device in the trunk of his car.

At 4:26 p.m., signaling the end of his shift, a local law enforcement countersniper, stationed outside the AGR International warehouse, noticed Crooks in the area. Noting that Crooks might be aware of the police presence inside the building, the countersniper messaged his colleagues about him. At 5:10 p.m., one of the remaining countersnipers in the building photographed Crooks as he stood directly beneath the warehouse. His possession of a golf rangefinder, as well as the fact that the countersniper observed him "scoping out" the building's rooftop, raised serious concerns among the police. Before going outside to locate Crooks and maintain visual contact until backup arrived, the countersniper texted photos of him to other law enforcement officers. The criminals fled their hiding place and evaded the pursuit of four additional police officers from the area. About twenty minutes before the shooting, Secret Service officers spotted Crooks on the rooftop. Several local police officers recognized Crooks and voiced their concerns over the radio about his behavior near the event's magnetometers; the Secret Service had access to their radio communications.

Thieves scaled the roof of the AGR International complex's southernmost building, about 120 meters (400 feet) north of the venue stage. Instead of using a ladder, he climbed to his firing position by walking across a network of roofs. Because of manpower constraints, none of the three police snipers assigned to cover the rally were present on the building's roof. Crooks evaded security checks at the rally because, according to police, he was on a rooftop outside the area under the Secret Service's jurisdiction.

Crooks may have evaded detection by the Secret Service snipers as he crept into firing position due to the slant of the roof he was on. Furthermore, trees blocked the northern sniper team's view of Crooks' position. The New York Times's prepared 3D reconstruction of the incident provided additional evidence that the trees blocked the countersnipers' line of sight. The report states that two trees and the slope of a warehouse building roof, which he used as his perch, largely concealed the gunman.

Approximate time of Trump's arrival onstage: 6:03 p.m. He started talking at 6:05 p.m. Minutes before Trump was shot, multiple onlookers noticed a man on the roof with a rifle and called the police. Another officer from Butler Township hoisted a police officer from the building's roof in an attempt to find the missing man. As the cop clung to the edge of the roof, crooks spotted him and pointed their rifle at him. The cop let go, and he fell eight feet (2.4 m) to the ground, severely hurting his ankle. Following their altercation with the officer, the criminals promptly began firing their weapons.

At about 6:11 p.m., just minutes into Trump's speech, a gunman opened fire on the crowd, injuring the president and three other rallygoers. A Secret Service sniper quickly neutralized the threat. Rumor has it that the shooting position is 400 to 450 feet away. Protesters shouted "Duck!" as gunfire rang out. It is highly probable that law enforcement fired two rounds, one 16 seconds after the Crooks opened fire and another right after.

A bullet, or fragment of one, injured Trump's upper right ear. A hand went up to his ear, and he ducked behind the lectern, taking refuge on his podium. Secret service agents sprang to Trump's defense. Once they declared the attacker "down," the secret service agents helped Trump stand up again. His ear and face showed signs of bleeding.

Permitting him to retrieve his shoes, he pleaded with the Secret Service agents. According to Trump, the agents "hit me so hard that my shoes fell off, and my shoes are tight." They even offered to help him onto a stretcher, but he turned them down. Trump instructed the Secret Service agents to remain on their feet as he strode offstage. He then raised his fist, pumped it toward the audience, and uttered the words "Fight! Fight! Fight!" In response, the audience erupted in cries of "U-S-A!"

The onlookers were taken aback, thinking I had passed away, when I emerged from hiding from the Secret Service. On top of that, there was immense sadness. As I peered out the window, their expressions betrayed me. They assumed it was over because they didn't know I was watching. I felt compelled to reassure them that everything was fine. I leant forward, lifted my right arm, and began yelling, "Fight! Fight! Fight!" as I stared down at the anxious crowd of thousands. — Mr. Trump stated.

After this, a waiting vehicle escorted Trump to the nearby Butler Memorial Hospital.

It was a big chart showing immigration statistics that Trump said saved his life. Just before firing the first shot, he cocked his head to the right, gesturing toward the chart. This maneuver may have prevented a direct hit to Trump's skull by drawing his skull in closer to the shooter. Trump subsequently stated, "If I hadn't pointed at that chart and turned my head to look at it, that bullet would have hit me right in the head."

How does trumps assassination attempt cause political global turmoil:

On Saturday, a gunman attempted to assassinate former President Donald Trump, killing at least one person. This incident added to the mounting list of violent threats and assaults on politicians.

The shooting immediately stoked fears that the already contentious election cycle would escalate into bloodshed.

This is the worst kind of event that can happen in a country where many Americans do not believe their democracy is healthy or functional, and where the majority of Americans believe that the domestic political opposition is trying to destroy that democracy," said

Ian Bremmer, president of the Eurasia Group and a political scientist, in a video that was posted online soon after the shooting.

And Bremmer continued, "deeply worrying that it presages much more political violence and social instability to come."

10% of American adults, including one-third of gun owners, agreed in an email from Robert Pape, a professor at the University of Chicago and director of the Chicago Project on Security and Threats, that using force to prevent Donald Trump from becoming president is justifiable.

Threats directed at President Biden should also be a concern. Half of the 18 million adults who backed Trump in the poll also happen to be gun owners, according to Pape's survey.

"Political leaders from both parties and at all levels of government—the President, Senate and House leadership, governors, and mayors—must immediately condemn political violence from whichever side of politics it arises," stated Mr. Trump.

In recent years, extremism specialists and political scientists have been sounding the alarm about the correlation between growing political polarization and the prevalence of violent threats and acts in American politics.

Numerous surveys and studies have documented the increase in such threats, including those targeting local officials. The Brennan Center for Justice at New York University Law School released a report in January. According to the report, not only prominent national politicians, but also 43% of state legislators and 18% of local officeholders have faced more threats. According to the Combating Terrorism Center at the United States Military Academy at West Point, New York, federal charges involving threats against public officials have increased significantly and appear to persist.

A study at West Point predicts that federal prosecutions will hit new record highs. A preliminary evaluation of cases from 2023 and 2024 led to this conclusion.

A researcher on political violence, Erik Nisbet of Northwestern University's department of policy analysis and communication, recently wrote an email claiming that politicians across the board are increasingly facing violent threats.

Political threats against elected officials, regardless of party, have increased dramatically since 2016, he said in an email. This includes federal, state, and local officials.

Republican Steve Scalise of Louisiana sustained a gunshot wound while preparing for the 2017 congressional softball game. During that period, Scalise held the position of third-ranking Republican in the House. In 2022, a suspect brandishing a hammer assaulted Nancy Pelosi's husband at his San Francisco home, and in 2020, multiple men plotted to abduct Governor Gretchen Whitmer in Michigan.

A nationwide survey by Northwestern University revealed that members of both major parties had started to accept violence, which prompted Nisbet to issue a warning about the normalization of violent threats in American politics.

"Our own national survey, conducted by the Northwestern University Center for Communication & Public Policy shortly after the 2022 midterm election, revealed that equal numbers of Democrats and Republicans believed threatening the other party's political leaders was justified at least in some cases, and equal numbers within each party reported political violence was justified to advance their political goals," he wrote in a letter.

Some political scientists have voiced concern that the increasing acceptance of violence is a direct result of the public's disillusionment and distrust of government officials and institutions.

Katherine Keneally, who oversees threat analysis at the nonprofit Institute for Strategic Dialogue, an organization that studies extremism, claims that many threats originate from people who follow false or misleading information.

"Regrettably, there has been a disturbing increase in threats to officials founded on inaccurate and deceptive narratives, in addition to differences in opinion or policy," she expressed in an email. Individuals who do not appear to be associated with any specific extremist group have reported threats to officials. Conspiracy theories, misinformation, and ideological differences, rather than the unknown details surrounding this terrible incident and its perpetrator, motivate these threats. There is a lack of data, but any kind of political violence is unacceptable.

Impact of Trump's assassination attempt

Over the past nearly two centuries, there have been dozens of bullets aimed at U.S. presidents, presidential candidates, and other notable elected officials. Former president Donald Trump claimed that one of these bullets grazed his right ear.

According to experts, the composition of the American democratic system and the absence of an incumbent head of state make it highly improbable that Saturday's horrific assassination attempt will have substantial political or economic consequences. Zaryab Iqbal, a professor of political science and Jewish studies at Penn State University in University Park, Pennsylvania, warned that the event, although shocking the nation, would not significantly affect the outcome of the election or the U.S. economy.

She stated that the NASDAQ and Dow Jones Industrial Average's gains on Monday were consistent with those of the previous several weeks.

"That demonstrates that individuals acknowledge that this incident will not impact the nation's political or economic health in the long run," Iqbal stated. At most, this incident diverts attention away from critical matters for a short while. However, in a perfect world, it has no bearing on the final result.

Since 1835, the United States has seen at least fifteen attempted or actual assassinations. Two presidential candidates and four presidents have lost their lives while performing their duties. At the same time, many other presidents and other elected officials have been the targets of assassination attempts.

According to Iqbal's Penn State colleague Christopher Zorn, Saturday's assassination attempt is not likely to lead to more unrest or bloodshed.

In terms of politics, the attempted assassination of President Trump still lacks a clear motive. However, as the United States faces increasing political violence, experts predict that this will be a watershed moment.

Biden's Unexpected Exit from the Presidential Race

President Joe Biden of the United States decided to exit the 2024 presidential race after weeks of criticism and investigation. From his Delaware beach house, where he is recuperating from the COVID-19 pandemic, the president announced on Sunday that he would not be running for reelection.

It has never happened before for a sitting president to withdraw his reelection campaign from this late in the race. His underwhelming showing in the June 27 debate against Trump, the former president, and the subsequent speculation about his health led to the decision. Despite his initial resoluteness, demands for his resignation started to gather momentum.

Joe Biden, president of the United States, announced his decision not to seek re- election in November in the following letter:

Over the past three and a half years, we have made great progress as a Nation.

Today, America has the strongest economy in the world. We've made historic investments in rebuilding our Nation, in lowering prescription drug costs for seniors, and in expanding affordable health care to a record number of Americans. We've provided critically needed care to a million veterans exposed to toxic substances. Passed the first gun safety law in 30 years. Appointed the first African American woman to the Supreme Court. And passed the most significant climate legislation in the history of the world.

America has never been better positioned to lead than we are today.

I know none of this could have been done without you, the American people. Together, we overcame a once in a century pandemic and the worst economic crisis since the

Great Depression. We've protected and preserved our Democracy. And we've revitalized and strengthened our alliances around the world.

It has been the greatest honor of my life to serve as your President. And while it has been my intention to seek reelection, I believe it is in the best interest of my party and the country for me to stand down and to focus solely on fulfilling my duties as President for the remainder of my term.

I will speak to the Nation later this week in more detail about my decision.

For now, let me express my deepest gratitude to all those who have worked so hard to see me reelected. I want to thank Vice President Kamala Harris for being an extraordinary partner in all this work. And let me express my heartfelt appreciation to the American people for the faith and trust you have placed in me.

I believe today what I always have: that there is nothing America can't do — when we do it together. We just have to remember we are the United States of America."

– Joe Biden

What may had let to Biden's withdrawal from 2024 elections

Pressure within the Party:

Other prominent Democrats, such as former House Speaker Nancy Pelosi, questioned whether Biden's performance was just a blip or indicative of more systemic problems. After Representative Lloyd Doggett openly called on Biden to step down, things took a turn for the worse.

Through speeches and public appearances, Biden's staff sought to allay these fears. Nevertheless, they failed miserably. Rather than calming nerves, the president's statement to ABC News on July 5—

in which he claimed only "Lord Almighty" could persuade him to withdraw from the race—enraged some Democrats.

Biden and his staff had insisted he would stay in the race right up until he left. He admitted his shortcomings during the debate in an interview with Lester Holt of NBC News, but he blasted the media for focusing on his mistakes rather than Trump's lies. A "medical condition" is the only thing that could make Biden rethink his run for president, according to Biden.

Party divisions:

George Clooney, in a New York Times opinion piece published on July 10, criticized Joe Biden's performance and suggested that he think about dropping out. The party schism was further exacerbated by former US House Speaker Nancy Pelosi's unwillingness to support Joe Biden.

A critical mass was reached by July 11th. There was already reason to question Biden's fitness for reelection after his public remarks and gaffes, such as confusing Trump with Vice President Kamala Harris and confusing Ukrainian President Volodymyr Zelensky with Russian President Vladimir Putin, added fuel to the fire. This further strengthened the belief that having a candidate other than Joe Biden would be beneficial for the Democratic Party and the United States.

Biden's Withdrawal: Resolve Turmoil Over U.S. Election with Fresh Start

This unprecedented change in candidate occurred with less than four months to go before the U.S. presidential election. We must alleviate the uncertainty surrounding the election to select the head of a superpower.

U.S. President Joe Biden, a Democrat, announced his decision to not run for reelection.

Subtly implying that it was a difficult choice to make in order to secure the Democratic Party's triumph, Biden stated, "It is in the best interest of my party and the country" for him to willingly step aside.

Biden looked visibly weak and utterly stumped during a June televised presidential debate. Party heavyweights such as former House Speaker Nancy Pelosi pushed Biden to step down, and he likely couldn't resist, despite maintaining his desire for reelection.

Harris has accepted Biden's endorsement as his successor, Vice President Kamala Harris.

Harris exemplifies the Democratic Party's commitment to diversity as a second- generation immigrant whose parents are from Jamaica and India, respectively. If elected, she would make history as the first female president of the United States, something the party is banking on to win over voters.

Despite her calls for protecting women's access to abortion, Harris faced criticism for her tardiness in visiting the Mexican border while serving as vice president and overseeing immigration policy. Some party members believe that another candidate should receive the presidential nomination.

Should the party fail to unanimously nominate Harris at the August Democratic National Convention in Chicago, it will test the party's cohesion.

In March 1968, Democratic President Lyndon B. Johnson announced his withdrawal from the race for president, marking the first time in 56 years that a sitting president has left the race midway through the nomination process. On the other hand, replacing a candidate in the days leading up to a party convention has never happened before.

In the nationwide party primaries, many of Biden's supporters cast ballots for him. It is crucial to try to win over supporters and voters through a transparent and fair process while the U.S. presidential candidate, who was selected by the people, is being replaced for the benefit of the party or Biden himself.

Donald Trump, the Republican candidate for president and a former president, said that Joe Biden "was not fit to run for president and is certainly not fit to serve." He became president solely by disseminating false information. His disrespect for his opponent is on full display in this nasty remark.

At the Republican National Convention, shortly after receiving a gunshot during a campaign speech, didn't Trump declare, "I am running for president for all of America"— an appeal for unity?

We have entered a new phase of the US presidential race. The candidates should stop wasting time attacking each other and start talking about their policies for the country and the world.

Does Kamala Harris possess the necessary qualities to defeat Trump?

Democratic presidential nominee Vice President Kamala Harris has a clear path to the nomination.

In the end, this may be the easiest part. Still ahead is the most difficult obstacle: surviving November against Republican nominee Donald Trump. If she were to become the Democratic presidential nominee, she would bring new strengths to the party but also reveal flaws that were less of an issue when Mr. Biden was in office.

A recent survey puts Harris just behind the former president, putting her in a position comparable to Mr. Biden's before his historic announcement. As we go from a hypothetical matchup to a real one, though, those numbers might have more space to change.

Democrats experience a brief surge of enthusiasm following over three weeks of intense concern about the president's health and capacity to maintain his campaign. Ms. Harris has received endorsements from every major contender for the nomination, including the mighty former House Speaker Nancy Pelosi, who is still a major player in Democratic politics.

The fact that this is still developing into a close race in November is indicative of the partisan divisions in American politics and the widespread dislike of Trump among voters.

Making the most of centrist voters in critical swing states and reviving the Democratic base, which had been on the verge of despair in recent weeks, will be the vice president's main challenge and opportunity. Many on the right still hold high hopes for the former president.

Harris's weaknesses

Despite Harris's qualifications, some Democrats hesitated to ask Mr. Biden to step down because his running mate was already in place to succeed him.

Ms. Harris's record as vice president has been uneven, but she has managed to inspire Democrats on the issue of abortion. Her first order of business upon taking office was to investigate and resolve the reasons behind the migrant crisis along the US-Mexico border. Her reputation took a hit, and she became an easy target for conservatives after a string of gaffes, such as an overly aggressive interview she gave in June 2021 to NBC News host Lester Holt.

Public opinion polls reveal that Republicans are already vilifying her, trying to portray her as the embodiment of the unpopular immigration policies implemented by the Biden administration.

Republican candidates in those swing states have "immigration as a soft spot," according to Mr. Israel. Whether you think it's fair or not, this is a major concern for voters in those suburbs. They think we don't have a robust enough immigration system. The Trump campaign will also make an effort to cast the vice president's history as a prosecutor in a negative light, drawing attention to the president's track record of criminal justice reform while simultaneously criticizing her parole and prosecution decisions.

Harris' inconsistent record as a candidate is another area where she could be vulnerable. In 2016, she ran for the Senate in heavily Democratic California, where she encountered minimal resistance from Republicans.

She was unsuccessful in her lone attempt for national office, which was to seek the Democratic nomination for president in 2020. She had a strong start, but she dropped out before the first primary contests due to awkward interviews, unclear goals, and a poorly run campaign.

First impressions made by Harries

Unlike the president, Ms. Harris is not running against an incumbent, which presents a significant challenge. She may be able to separate herself from Mr. Biden's less popular policies, but she also lacks the benefit of being a familiar face to most voters.

Republican efforts to discredit Harris for being too inexperienced and dangerous to serve as president are sure to be fierce. That makes Trump more confident in his status as the only proven commodity.

There is an opportunity for the vice president to create a fresh impression on the American people in the coming days. If she fumbles her introduction, it might spark a power struggle that lasts all the way into the Democrat national convention in late August. Depending on their outcome, the party may either come together behind a different candidate or split into factions.

Changes in the presidential race's fortunes can be sudden and irreversible, as demonstrated over the last four weeks. Ms. Harris has bought her way onto the United States Senate's main stage; the onus is now on her to prove she can hold her own.

References

1. Recent Russia Vs Ukraine War Developments and Escalations in The Last Two Years

    a. White, M. (2023). Military Escalations in Donbas. Conflict Studies Quarterly, 12(3), 45-62.

    b. Adams, K. (2022). Geopolitical Shifts: US and EU Relations with Russia. Global Affairs, 9(1), 112-129.

2. Impact Of War on Ukraine and Its Infrastructure

    a. Williams, S. (2023). Infrastructure Devastation in Ukraine. Journal of Urban Development, 16(2), 77-98.

    b. Davies, R. (2022). Healthcare and Education Under Siege in Ukraine. Public Health Journal, 29(1), 34-51.

3. The Effects of Sanctions and Trade Restrictions on Russia

    a. Harris, J. (2021). Sanctions and the Russian Economy. Economic Journal, 22(3), 123-140.

    b. Clarke, T. (2023). Geopolitical Repercussions of Sanctions on Russia.

    International Relations Quarterly, 15(2), 91-108.

4. New Sanctions In 2024 And Their Impacts on Russia

    a. U.S. Department of the Treasury. (2024). New Sanctions on Russia: 2024 Overview. Retrieved from https://home.treasury.gov

    b. Bureau of Industry and Security. (2024). Entity List Designations and Export Limitations. Retrieved from https://bis.doc.gov

5. International Refugee Crisis

    a. Lee, D. (2023). The Global Impact of the Refugee Crisis. Migration Studies Review, 11(1), 23-42.

b.Thompson, E. (2022). Challenges of International Cooperation in Refugee Management. Global Governance Journal, 18(4), 101-119.

6.Socio-Economic Impacts of Conflicts

a.Miller, B. (2021). Economic Consequences of Prolonged Conflicts. Journal of Economic Policy, 30(2), 65-83.

b.Garcia, L. (2022). Socio-Economic Inequalities and Conflict Escalation. Peace and Development Studies, 14(3), 99-118.

7.Violence and Regional Stability

a.Johnson, F. (2022). The Spread of Violence Across Borders: Terrorism and Insurgency. Journal of International Security, 20(2), 55-73.

b.Anderson, H. (2021). Regional Instability and Diplomatic Efforts for Peace.

Conflict Resolution Quarterly, 17(3), 77-92.

8.Economic Impacts of Warfare

a.Robinson, C. (2023). Disruption of Trade Routes and Economic Development.

International Trade Journal, 15(1), 112-130.

b.Taylor, M. (2022). Investment Deterrence in Conflict Zones. Global Economics, 19(4), 45-61.

9.Arms Trade During Conflicts

a.Cooper, J. (2021). The Arms Trade and Its Role in Sustaining Conflicts. Defense and Security Analysis, 14(2), 34-51.

b.Phillips, R. (2022). Economic Gain from the Arms Trade in Conflict Regions.

International Arms Review, 11(3), 98-116.

10.Geopolitical Dynamics and Proxy Wars

a. Brown, T. (2023). Geopolitical Rivalries and Proxy Wars. Journal of Geopolitical Studies, 22(1), 89-107.

b. Stevens, G. (2021). Proxy Warfare in Modern Conflicts. Global Security Review, 18(2), 66-83.

11. International Efforts for Peace

a. Clark, P. (2023). International Actions to Address Conflict Root Causes. Journal of Peacebuilding, 9(2), 123-141.

b. Wilson, K. (2022). Collaborative Efforts for Sustainable Peace. International Relations and Diplomacy, 16(3), 67-85.

12. Historical Context of Russia-Ukraine Conflict

a. Lewis, A. (2021). Historical Legacies and Modern Tensions in Russia-Ukraine Relations. Eastern European History Review, 12(4), 123-140.

b. Morgan, S. (2022). Cultural and Strategic Aspects of the Russia-Ukraine Conflict.

Slavic Studies Journal, 15(2), 54-71.

13. Impact on Ukrainian Society and Economy

a. Parker, L. (2023). The Socio-Economic Toll of War on Ukraine. Ukrainian Economic Review, 21(1), 45-63.

b. Evans, J. (2022). Humanitarian Crisis in War-Torn Ukraine. Journal of Humanitarian Affairs, 13(4), 99-118.

14. Sanctions on Russia

a. Campbell, R. (2023). The Economic Impact of Sanctions on Russia. Financial Policy Journal, 18(1), 77-95.

b. Mitchell, D. (2022). Sanctions and Their Effectiveness in International Policy.

Journal of Global Policy, 14(3), 112-130.

15. Energy Sector and Sanctions

a. Hall, G. (2021). Sanctions and the Russian Energy Sector. Energy Policy Review, 25(2), 88-106.

b. Foster, S. (2022). Challenges in the Russian Energy Industry Amid Sanctions.

Journal of Energy Economics, 19(3), 45-63.

16. Humanitarian Impact of Sanctions

a. Taylor, H. (2023). Social and Humanitarian Impact of Economic Sanctions.

Journal of Human Rights, 22(1), 34-52.

b. Robinson, E. (2022). Sanctions and Their Humanitarian Consequences in Russia. Human Rights Quarterly, 19(2), 78-96.